# Everyday Home Improvements
## Volume II

*Complete Handyman's Library*™
Handyman Club of America
Minneapolis, Minnesota

Published in 1994 by
Handyman Club of America
12301 Whitewater Drive
Minnetonka, Minnesota  55343

Published by arrangement with Cy DeCosse Incorporated
ISBN 0-86573-742-8

Printed on American paper by
R. R. Donnelley & Sons Co. (0894)

CREDITS:
*Created by:* The Editors of Cy DeCosse Incorporated in
cooperation with Black & Decker. **BLACK&DECKER**
is a trademark of Black & Decker (US), Incorporated and is
used under license.

# Contents

# Introduction

Your house is full of plumbing and electrical appliances, fixtures, and other devices that make your life relaxing, enjoyable, or easier. Most of these items receive heavy daily usage and, therefore, you often need to make plumbing or electrical repairs. *Everyday Home Improvements: Volume II* provides all the information you need to make these repairs and keep your house functioning smoothly and safely. It gives you clear step-by-step instructions and tells you all about the tools and materials needed to make these repairs quickly and safely.

The first half of the book covers basic plumbing repairs and replacements. Essential plumbing tools, as well as specialty tools made for particular plumbing repairs, are presented and their use demonstrated. Many of these tools can be found at rental centers, saving you the cost of purchasing a tool you may only need once.

All of the common faucet types are represented in a section on fixing leaky faucets. You learn how to repair the faucet valves as well as how to replace the entire faucet if that is what is required. This section includes information on repairing sprayers, installing shutoff valves, fixing 2-handle and 3-handle tub/shower faucets and the shower heads, replacing sillcocks, and repairing hose bibs.

Common Toilet Problems contains everything you need to know about maintaining and repairing your toilet, including how to remove an old toilet and install a new one. How to clear a clogged toilet is shown in the next section, Cleaning Clogs and Fixing Drains. You also see how to clear clogged sinks, shower drains, tub drains, drain traps, floor drains and main and branch drain lines. Then you learn how to fix leaky sink strainers and tub drains.

The last section in the plumbing half of the book demonstrates how to fix gas and electric water heaters, how to make both emergency and permanent repairs on burst or frozen pipes, and how to quiet noisy pipes.

The second half of the book covers the tools, materials, and techniques necessary to make basic electrical repairs. You also learn how to work with electricity safely, so that you can make any repair with confidence. A glossary of electrical terms is provided to make all the information very clear.

The first section presents everything you need to know about the elements in your electrical system and how to work with them, whether you have fuses or circuit breakers. You learn about the different types of wire and cable you may find in your house, how a service panel functions, and how the entire system works together to provide you with power for the many appliances and fixtures in your home.

Then a series of sections provides you with information on how to repair and install wall switches, receptacles, incandescent and fluorescent fixtures (including recessed lights), doorbells, and thermostats. You also learn how to fix a lamp by replacing the socket or cord plug.

Throughout *Everyday Home Improvements: Volume II* you will find solutions to your repair problems. The troubleshooting charts will be particularly helpful in determining exactly which repair you need to make. And the step-by-step instructions will help give you successful, professional-quality results.

# Basic Plumbing Know-how

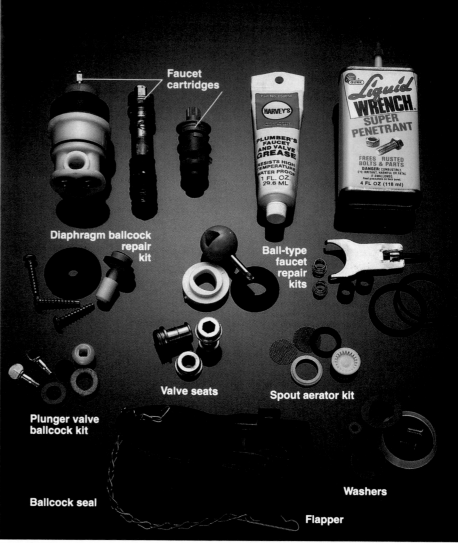

Faucet cartridges

Diaphragm ballcock repair kit

Ball-type faucet repair kits

Valve seats

Spout aerator kit

Plunger valve ballcock kit

Ballcock seal

Flapper

Washers

**Materials** for Plumbing

**Tools** for Plumbing ▶

The plumbing lines running through your home include two separate systems of pipes. The **freshwater supply** pipes are narrow, ½ to 1 inch in diameter, feeding clean water to all parts of your house under pressure. The **drain-waste-vent** (DWV) lines run through large pipes, 1¼ inches or more in diameter, into the sewer. The drain system is under no pressure; it operates by the force of gravity.

Nearly all plumbing repairs involve **leaks** or **clogs**. Leaks are caused by the pressure in the supply system which puts stress on the pipes, joints and fixtures. Clogs form because of the lack of pressure in the drain system.

The following pages introduce the basic plumbing techniques. The first rule of successful plumbing repair: shut off the water and drain the pipes before beginning.

## How to Shut Off the Water & Drain the Pipes

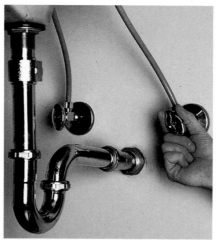

**Individual shutoff valves** are found on some sinks and most toilets. They are generally located at the supply tubes feeding the fixture. Turn the valve clockwise to stop water flow, then open a faucet or flush the toilet to release water standing in the lines.

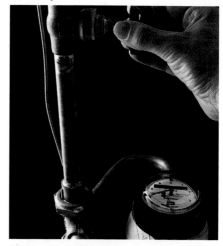

**Main shutoff valve**, located near water meter, can be closed to shut off all water. Open faucets at the highest and lowest points in your home to drain water lines.

**Hacksaw**

**Pipe wrench**

**Ratchet & deep socket**

**Stiff wire brush**

**Channel-type pliers**

**Drain auger**

**Allen wrenches**

**Flanged plunger**

**Closet auger**

**Seat-dressing tool**

**Expansion nozzle**

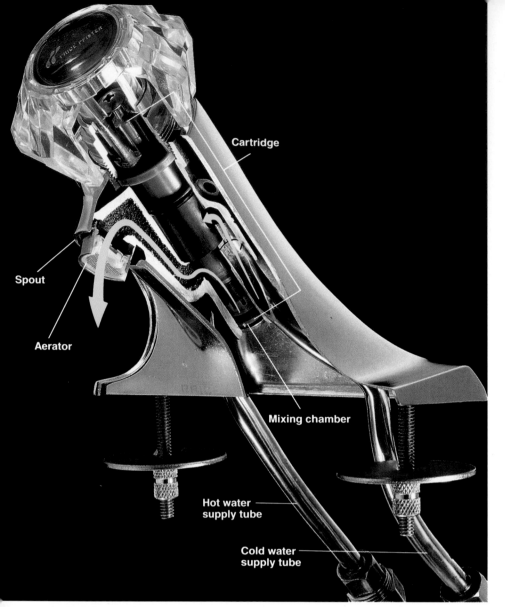

Cartridge

Spout

Aerator

Mixing chamber

Hot water
supply tube

Cold water
supply tube

**Typical faucet** has a single handle attached to a hollow cartridge. The cartridge controls hot and cold water flowing from the supply tubes into the mixing chamber. Water is forced out the spout and through the aerator. When repairs are needed, replace the entire cartridge.

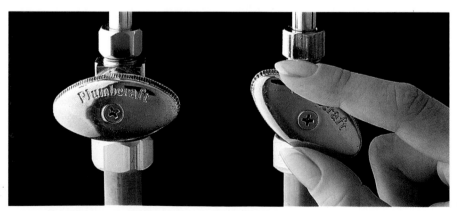

**Turn off water** before starting any faucet repair, using shutoff valves underneath faucet, or main service valve found near water meter (page 6). When opening shutoff valves after finishing repairs, keep faucet handle in open position to release trapped air. When water runs steadily, close faucet.

# Making Faucet Repairs

A leaky faucet is the most common home plumbing problem. Fixing leaks is easy, but the techniques for making repairs will vary, depending on the design of the faucet. Before beginning work, you must first identify your faucet design and determine what replacement parts are needed.

There are four basic faucet designs: ball-type, two types of cartridge (disc and sleeve) and compression. Many faucets can be identified easily by outer appearance, but others must be taken apart before the design can be recognized (page 11).

The compression design is used in many double-handle faucets. Compression faucets all have washers or seals that must be replaced from time to time. These repairs are easy to make, and replacement parts are inexpensive, though you may need to take the valve stem with you to the hardware store to make certain you get the proper sized replacements.

Ball-type, and the two cartridge type faucets are all known as washerless faucets. Many washerless faucets are controlled with a single handle, although some cartridge models use two handles. Washerless faucets are more trouble-free than compression faucets, and are designed for quick repair.

# Faucet Problems & Repairs

Most faucet problems are easy to fix. You can save money and time by making these simple repairs yourself. Replacement parts for faucet repairs usually are inexpensive and readily available at hardware stores and home centers. Techniques for repair vary, depending on the faucet design (page 11).

If a badly worn faucet continues to leak, even after repairs are made, the faucet should be replaced. In less than an hour, you can replace an old, problem faucet with a new model that is designed to provide years of trouble-free service.

| Problems | Repairs |
| --- | --- |
| Faucet drips from the end of the spout, or leaks around the base. | Identify the faucet design (page 11), then install replacement parts, using directions on following pages. |
| Old, worn-out faucet continues to leak after repairs are made. | Replace the old faucet (pages 18 to 21). |
| Water pressure at spout seems low, or water flow is partially blocked. | Clean faucet aerator (page 24). |
| Water pressure from sprayer seems low, or sprayer leaks from handle. | 1. Clean sprayer head (page 24).<br>2. Fix diverter valve (page 25). |
| Water leaks onto floor underneath faucet. | 1. Replace cracked sprayer hose (page 25).<br>2. Tighten water connections, or replace supply tubes and shutoff valves (pages 22 to 23).<br>3. Fix leaky sink strainer (page 53). |
| Hose bib or valve drips from spout or leaks around handle. | Take valve apart and replace washers and O-rings (pages 34 to 35). |

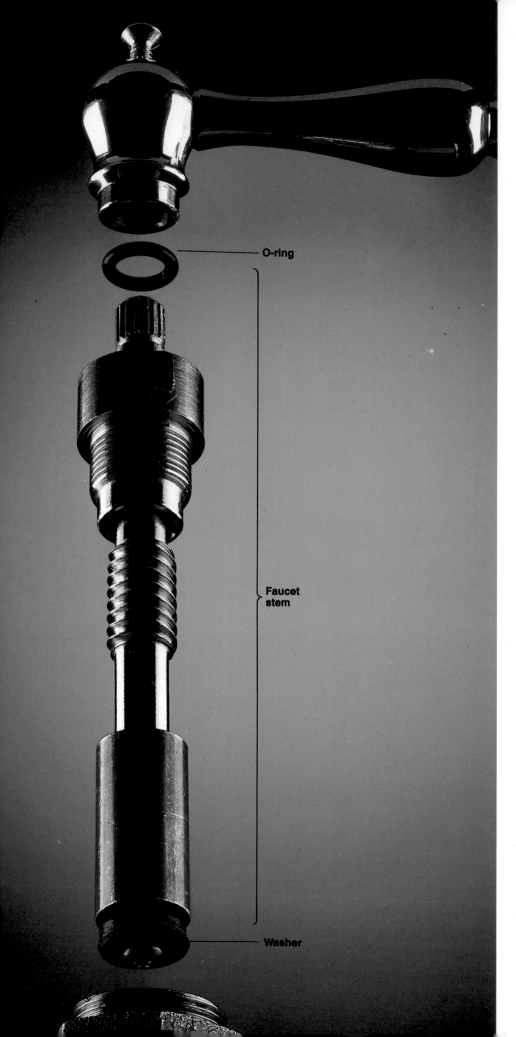

O-ring

Faucet
stem

Washer

# Fixing a Leaky Faucet

When faucets leak, it is usually because the washers, O-rings or seals are dirty, worn or cracked.

As you take a faucet apart, work carefully and pay attention to the arrangement of the parts. When installing new faucet parts, make sure the replacements match the original parts. Replacement parts for popular washerless faucets are identified by brand name and model number. To ensure a correct selection, you may want to bring the worn parts to the store for comparison.

### Before You Start:

**Tools & Materials for Ball-type Faucets:** channel-type pliers, faucet repair kit(s), utility knife, screwdriver.

**Tools & Materials for Disc-type Faucets:** allen wrench, screwdriver, cartridge.

**Tools & Materials for Sleeve-type Faucets:** screwdriver, channel-type pliers, needle-nose pliers, cartridge, O-rings, heatproof grease.

**Tools & Materials for Compression (stem and seat) Faucets:** screwdriver, adjustable wrench, washers, O-rings or string packing, utility knife, heatproof grease, seat wrench, seat-dressing tool, valve seats.

# How to Identify Your Faucet

**Cartridge faucets,** available in many styles, are washerless. They use cartridge inserts that contain all mechanical parts. The handle screw is hidden under an index cap on the collar. The two common types of cartridges are the disc-type and the sleeve-type.
**Replacement part** for cartridge faucet is a new cartridge. Do not try to replace the cartridge O-rings or seals. To fix a leaky cartridge faucet, see pages 14 to 15.

**Ball-type faucets** have a rounded collar on the single-lever handle. Underneath the collar is a dome-shaped cap. The handle is usually held to the faucet by a setscrew located in the collar. Inside, a hollow metal or plastic ball controls the water volume and temperature.
**Replacement parts** for a ball-type faucet are usually found in two separate repair kits, one containing valve seats and springs, the other including ball, cam and cam washer. Sometimes all these parts are included in a single kit. To fix a leaky ball-type faucet, see page 13.

**Compression faucets** (stem and seat) on many double-handle sink and tub fixtures have neoprene washers that compress against a valve seat. Index caps on top of faucet handles may conceal the handle screws.
**Replacement parts** for compression faucet include washer, and O-ring (or packing washer or packing string on older faucets). To fix a leaky compression faucet, see pages 16 to 17.

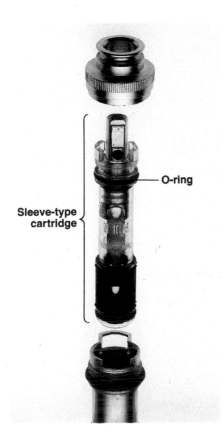

Sleeve-type cartridge

O-ring

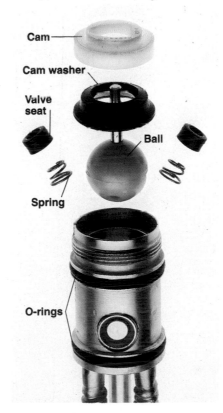

Cam

Cam washer

Valve seat

Ball

Spring

O-rings

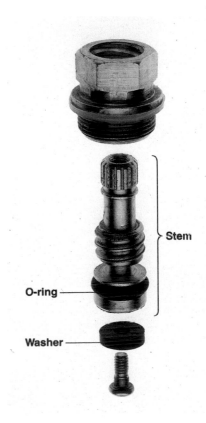

Stem

O-ring

Washer

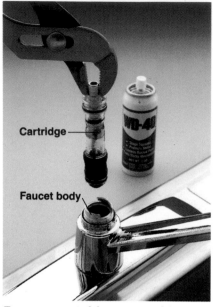

**Avoid scratches** to chrome by wrapping masking tape around the jaws of pliers or wrench. On double-handle faucets, repair one side at a time to avoid mismatching hot and cold stems.

**If the slots** on a stem washer are damaged by a screwdriver, deepen the screw slots with a hacksaw. If head of screw breaks, pry out the washer and twist the screw out with a needlenose pliers.

**Remove a stubborn cartridge** by gripping top of stem with channel-type pliers and lifting with a gentle back-and-forth motion. Applying penetrating oil may help. Be careful not to bend the cartridge or damage the faucet body.

**Clean spout attachments** if water pressure seems low, or if spray pattern is uneven. Separate all parts and clean off mineral deposits with a brush, then soak all parts overnight in lime-dissolving solution before reassembling. You may choose to replace rather than clean inexpensive aerator and spout attachments.

**Replace a faucet** if it continues to leak. Replacement fixtures come with detailed instructions, but you will need to know measurements to make a proper purchase. Write down on-center measurement between tailpieces, or bring the old faucet along when shopping for a replacement.

# How to Fix a Leaky Ball-type Faucet

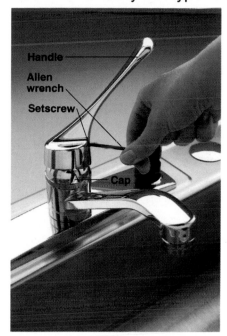

**1** Shut off water supply (page 8). Loosen handle setscrew with an allen wrench (or use the setscrew key included in purchased repair kit). Remove handle to expose adjusting ring located on the cap.

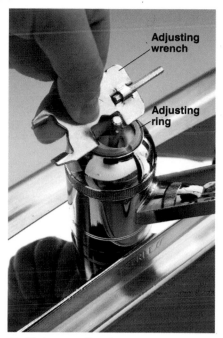

**2** Tighten adjusting ring with adjusting wrench included in the repair kit. (On some models, use channel-type pliers to tighten cap.) Reattach the handle, and turn on water. If faucet still leaks, turn off water again and remove the faucet handle.

**3** Unscrew cap with channel-type pliers. (Cover jaws of pliers with masking tape or heavy fabric to avoid scratching surface of cap.) Lift out the cam, cam washer and the rotating ball.

**4** Reach into faucet with screwdriver and remove valve seats and springs. Purchase new valve seats, springs, rotating ball, cam and cam washer, available in repair kits.

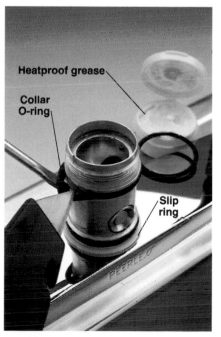

**5** Remove spout by twisting upward. Cut old O-rings off with a knife. Coat new O-rings with heatproof grease and install. Reinstall spout, pressing down until collar rests on plastic slip ring.

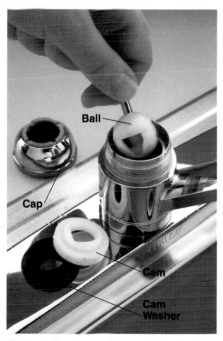

**6** Install new springs and valve seats, and new ball, cam washer and cam. Reassemble faucet.

## How to Fix a Leaky Cartridge Faucet (Disc-type)

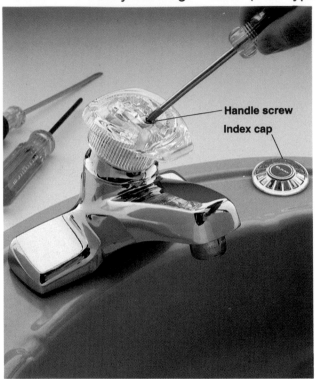

**1** Shut off the water supply (page 8). Pry off the index cap and remove the handle screw underneath. Remove the faucet handle.

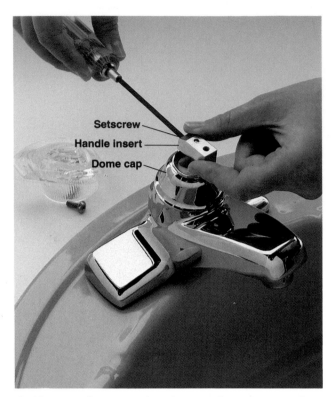

**2** Use an allen wrench to loosen the setscrew, then remove the handle insert. Unscrew and lift off the dome cap.

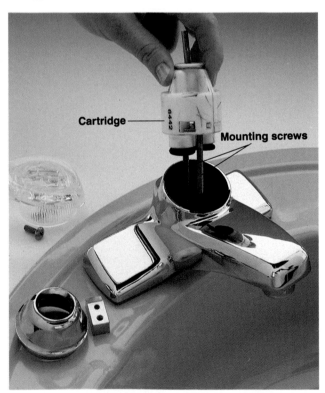

**3** Remove mounting screws that hold cartridge in faucet. Lift out cartridge. Purchase a new cartridge that matches the old cartridge.

**4** Lower the new cartridge into the faucet body, and replace the mounting screws. Screw on the dome cap. Replace the handle insert, handle and index cap.

## How to Fix a Leaky Cartridge Faucet (Sleeve-type)

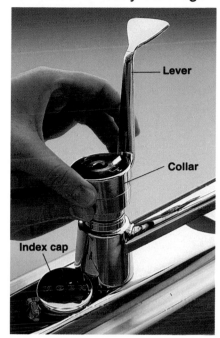

**1** Shut off water supply (page 8). Pry off index cap covering collar and remove the handle screw underneath. Lift the lever to the uppermost position to free inner lever from lip of retaining nut. Lift handle off.

**2** Remove the retaining nut using channel-type pliers. (On some bathroom faucets, you must also remove a grooved collar under the retaining nut.)

**3** Pry the retaining clip from the top of cartridge using needle-nose pliers.

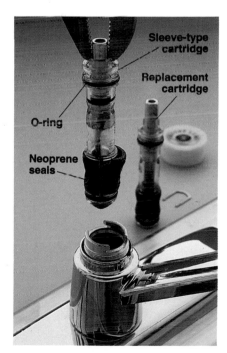

**4** Grip top of the cartridge with channel-type pliers. Pull straight up to remove cartridge. Bring old cartridge along when shopping for a replacement. Insert the new cartridge, and install the retaining clip.

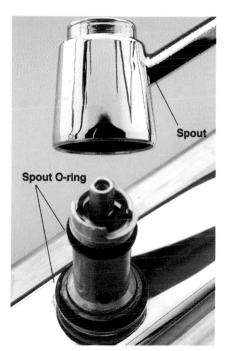

**5** Remove spout by pulling up and twisting. Cut off old O-rings using a knife. Spread heatproof grease on new O-rings before installing. Replace spout and retaining nut.

**6** Lift handle lever while holding collar tightly. Holding collar at an angle, slip flat edge of inner lever over the lip of retaining nut. Replace the handle screw and index cap.

# How to Fix a Leaky Compression (Stem and Seat) Faucet

**1** Shut off water supply (page 8). Remove the screw holding handle to faucet. (Screw may be hidden under index cap.) Remove handle. If handle sticks, apply penetrating oil and rock handle gently while pulling.

**2** Use an adjustable wrench or channel-type pliers to loosen the retaining nut (or packing nut on older faucets). Remove retaining nut by hand, then remove stem from faucet body.

**3** Unscrew brass stem screw, and pry out old washer. Replace washer with an exact duplicate. If brass screw shows signs of wear, replace it also. Repair kits include a wide assortment of washers and brass screws.

**4** Cut O-ring off stem using a knife. Install duplicate O-ring. Smear heatproof grease on all moving parts, including handle socket. Examine the valve seat (page opposite). If it is pitted, replace or dress valve seat before reassembling faucet.

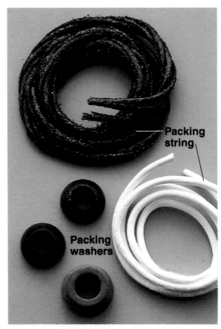

**On older faucets,** packing washer or self-forming packing string, found just under the packing nut, is used instead of O-rings. Replace packing washer; or hold stem with packing nut facing you, and wrap 5 or 6 loops of packing string clockwise around stem under packing nut.

**Washer variations:** A tophat stem faucet uses a tophat-shaped diaphragm. Simply pop a new diaphragm washer over the stem tip to fix leaks. A reverse-pressure stem uses a beveled washer that fits with beveled side facing the stem body.

## How to Remove a Wall-mounted Compression Faucet

**1** For double-handle compression faucets mounted on the wall, remove handle using the same method as for sink faucets (page opposite). Remove escutcheon from fitting. Escutcheon may be held with setscrew.

**2** Remove bonnet nut using reversible ratchet and deep socket. (Trim back wall tile and chip out plaster or concrete around nut, if necessary.) If nut sticks, apply penetrating oil and wait 15 minutes.

**3** Remove and replace stem washer. Remove and replace old O-ring, old packing washer or packing string. Lubricate stem lightly with heatproof grease, then reassemble faucet.

## How to Replace or Dress a Worn Valve Seat

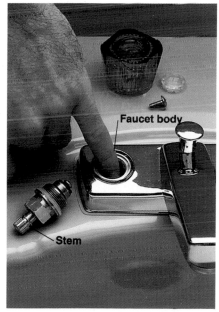

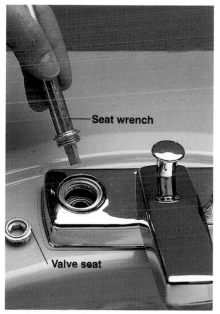

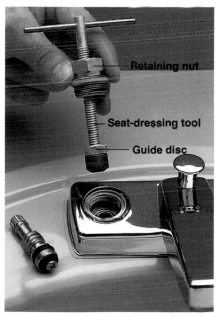

**1** Continuing leaks could mean that a brass valve seat inside the faucet body is damaged. Remove faucet stem and feel valve seat with a fingertip. If rough, replace the seat, or resurface it with a seat-dressing tool (right).

**2** Remove a deteriorated valve seat using seat wrench. Select end of wrench that fits valve seat and insert into faucet. Turn counterclockwise to remove. Use wrench to insert new seat. If the seat cannot be removed, resurface using a seat-dressing tool (right).

**To dress** (resurface) a valve seat, select a guide disc to fit faucet. Attach disc to dressing tool and insert through retaining nut. Tighten retaining nut lightly into faucet. Press tool down lightly and turn grinder clockwise. Seat is dressed when tool turns easily.

17

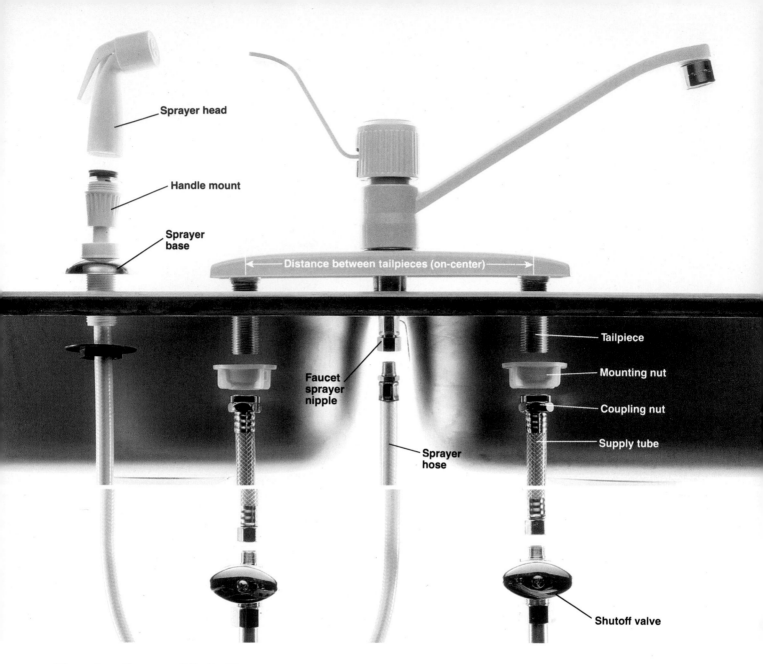

Sprayer head

Handle mount

Sprayer base

Distance between tailpieces (on-center)

Tailpiece

Mounting nut

Faucet sprayer nipple

Coupling nut

Supply tube

Sprayer hose

Shutoff valve

# Replacing a Sink Faucet

Installing a new faucet is an easy project that takes about one hour. Before buying a new faucet, first find the diameter of the sink openings, and measure the distance between the tailpieces (measured on-center). Make sure the tailpieces of the new faucet match the sink openings.

When shopping for a new faucet, choose a model made by a reputable manufacturer. Replacement parts for a well-known brand will be easy to find if the faucet ever needs repairs. Better faucets have solid brass bodies. They are easy to install and provide years of trouble-free service. Some washerless models have lifetime warranties.

Always install new supply tubes when replacing a faucet. Old supply tubes should not be reused. If

water pipes underneath the sink do not have shut-off valves, you may choose to install the valves while replacing the faucet (pages 22 to 23).

**Remember to turn off the water before beginning work (page 8).**

### Everything You Need:

Tools: basin wrench or channel-type pliers, putty knife, caulk gun, adjustable wrenches.

Materials: penetrating oil, silicone caulk or plumber's putty, two flexible supply tubes.

## How to Remove an Old Sink Faucet

**Mounting nut**

**Coupling nut**

**1** Spray penetrating oil on tailpiece mounting nuts and supply tube coupling nuts. Remove the coupling nuts with a basin wrench or channel-type pliers.

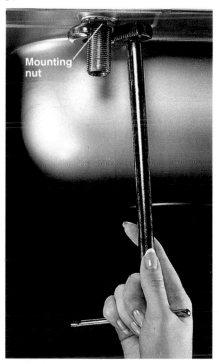

**Mounting nut**

**2** Remove the tailpiece mounting nuts with a basin wrench or channel-type pliers. Basin wrench has a long handle that makes it easy to work in tight areas.

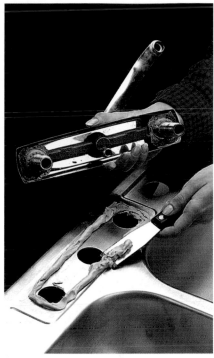

**3** Remove faucet. Use a putty knife to clean away old putty from surface of sink.

## Faucet Hookup Variations

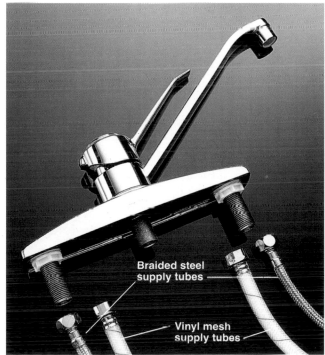

**Braided steel supply tubes**

**Vinyl mesh supply tubes**

**New faucet without supply tubes:** Buy two supply tubes. Supply tubes are available in braided steel or vinyl mesh (shown above), PB plastic, or chromed copper (page 22).

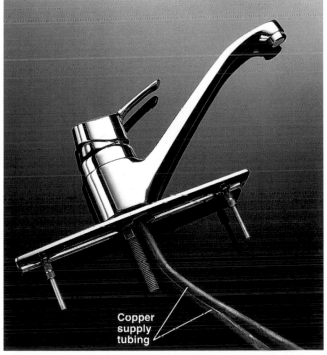

**Copper supply tubing**

**New faucet with preattached copper supply tubing:** Make water connections by attaching the supply tubing directly to the shutoff valves with compression fittings (page 21).

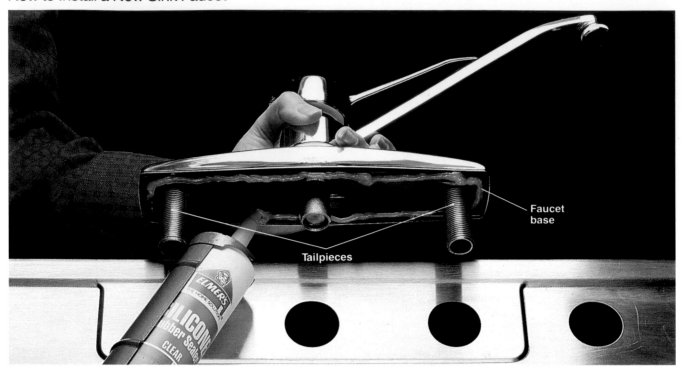

Faucet base

Tailpieces

**1** Apply a ¼" bead of silicone caulk or plumber's putty around the base of the faucet. Insert the faucet tailpieces into the sink openings. Position the faucet so base is parallel to back of sink, and press the faucet down to make sure caulk forms a good seal.

Friction washer

Mounting nut

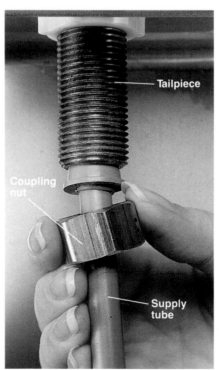

Tailpiece

Coupling nut

Supply tube

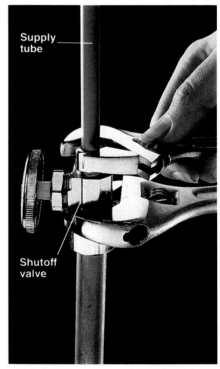

Supply tube

Shutoff valve

**2** Screw the metal friction washers and the mounting nuts onto the tailpieces, then tighten with a basin wrench or channel-type pliers. Wipe away excess caulk around base of faucet.

**3** Connect flexible supply tubes to faucet tailpieces. Tighten coupling nuts with a basin wrench or channel-type pliers.

**4** Attach supply tubes to shutoff valves, using compression fittings. Hand-tighten nuts, then use an adjustable wrench to tighten nuts ¼ turn. If necessary, hold valve with another wrench while tightening.

# How to Connect a Faucet with Preattached Supply Tubing

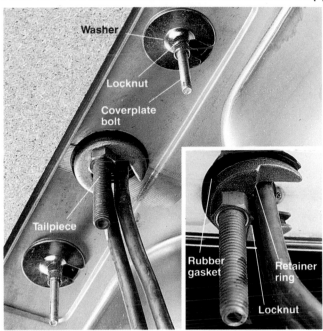

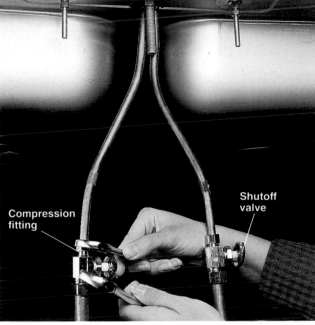

**1** Attach faucet to sink by placing rubber gasket, retainer ring, and locknut onto threaded tailpiece. Tighten locknut with a basin wrench or channel-type pliers. Some center-mounted faucets have a decorative coverplate. Secure coverplate from underneath with washers and locknuts screwed onto coverplate bolts.

**2** Connect preattached supply tubing to shutoff valves with compression fittings. Red-coded tube should be attached to the hot water pipe, blue-coded tube to the cold water pipe.

# How to Attach a Sink Sprayer

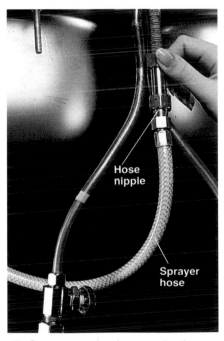

**1** Apply a ¼" bead of plumber's putty or silicone caulk to bottom edge of sprayer base. Insert tailpiece of sprayer base into sink opening.

**2** Place friction washer over tailpiece. Screw the mounting nut onto tailpiece and tighten with a basin wrench or channel-type pliers. Wipe away excess putty around base of sprayer.

**3** Screw sprayer hose onto the hose nipple on the bottom of the faucet. Tighten ¼ turn, using a basin wrench or channel-type pliers.

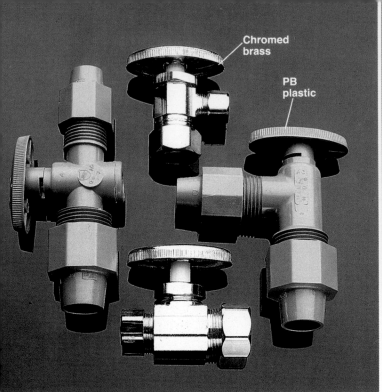

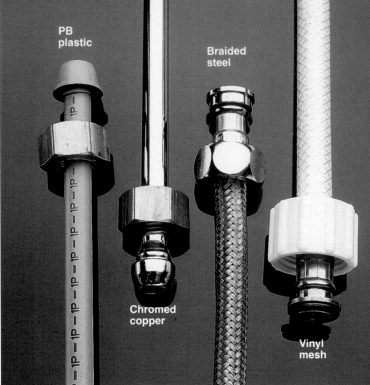

**Shutoff valves** allow you to shut off the water to an individual fixture so it can be repaired. They can be made from durable chromed brass or lightweight plastic. Shutoff valves come in ½" and ¾" diameters to match common water pipe sizes.

**Supply tubes** are used to connect water pipes to faucets, toilets, and other fixtures. They come in 12", 20", and 30" lengths. PB plastic and chromed copper tubes are inexpensive. Braided steel and vinyl mesh supply tubes are easy to install.

# Installing Shutoff Valves & Supply Tubes

Worn-out shutoff valves or supply tubes can cause water to leak underneath a sink or other fixture. First, try tightening the fitting with an adjustable wrench. If this does not fix the leak, replace the shutoff valves and supply tubes.

Shutoff valves are available in several fitting types. For copper pipes, valves with compression-type fittings are easiest to install. For plastic pipes, use grip-type valves. For galvanized iron pipes, use valves with female threads.

Older plumbing systems often were installed without fixture shutoff valves. When repairing or replacing plumbing fixtures, you may want to install shutoff valves if they are not already present.

## Everything You Need:

Tools: hacksaw, tubing cutter, adjustable wrench, tubing bender, felt-tipped pen.

Materials: shutoff valves, supply tubes, pipe joint compound.

## How to Install Shutoff Valves & Supply Tubes

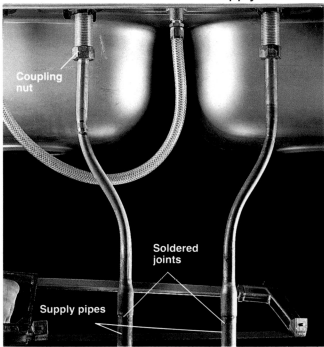

**1** Turn off water at the main shutoff valve (page 6). Remove old supply pipes. If pipes are soldered copper, cut them off just below the soldered joint, using a hacksaw or tubing cutter. Make sure the cuts are straight. Unscrew the coupling nuts, and discard the old pipes.

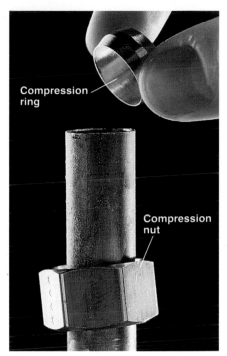

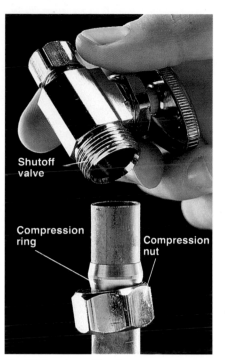

**2** Slide a compression nut and compression ring over copper water pipe. Threads of nut should face end of pipe.

**3** Slide shutoff valve onto pipe. Apply a layer of pipe joint compound to compression ring. Screw the compression nut onto the shutoff valve and tighten with an adjustable wrench.

**4** Bend chromed copper supply tube to reach from the tailpiece of the fixture to the shutoff valve, using a tubing bender. Bend the tube slowly to avoid crimping the metal.

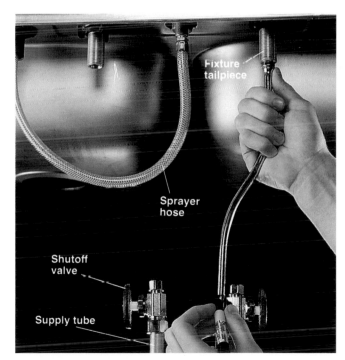

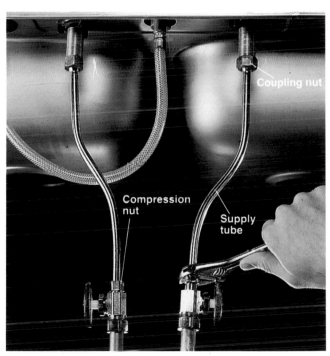

**5** Position the supply tube between fixture tailpiece and shutoff valve, and mark tube to length. Cut supply tube.

**6** Attach bell-shaped end of supply tube to fixture tailpiece with coupling nut, then attach other end to shutoff valve with compression ring and nut. Tighten all fittings with adjustable wrench.

# Fixing Sprayers & Aerators

If water pressure from a sink sprayer seems low, or if water leaks from the handle, it is usually because lime buildup and sediment have blocked small openings inside the sprayer head. To fix the problem, first take the sprayer head apart and clean the parts. If cleaning the sprayer head does not help, the problem may be caused by a faulty diverter valve. The diverter valve inside the faucet body shifts water flow from the faucet spout to the sprayer when the sprayer handle is pressed. Cleaning or replacing the diverter valve may fix water pressure problems.

Whenever making repairs to a sink sprayer, check the sprayer hose for kinks or cracks. A damaged hose should be replaced.

If water pressure from a faucet spout seems low, or if the flow is partially blocked, take the spout aerator apart and clean the parts. The aerator is a screw-on attachment with a small wire screen that mixes tiny air bubbles into the water flow. Make sure the wire screen is not clogged with sediment and lime buildup. If water pressure is low throughout the house, it may be because galvanized iron water pipes are corroded. Corroded pipes should be replaced.

**Everything You Need:**

Tools: screwdriver, channel-type pliers, needle-nose pliers, small brush.

Materials: vinegar, universal washer kit, heat-proof grease, replacement sprayer hose.

**Clean faucet aerators and sink sprayers** to fix most low water pressure problems. Take aerator or sprayer head apart, then use a small brush dipped in vinegar to remove sediment.

## How to Fix a Diverter Valve

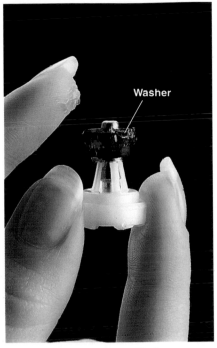

Washer

Diverter valve

**1** Shut off the water (page 8). Remove the faucet handle and the spout (see directions for your faucet type, pages 11 to 21).

**2** Pull diverter valve from faucet body with needlenose pliers. Use a small brush dipped in vinegar to clean lime buildup and debris from valve.

**3** Replace any worn O-rings or washers, if possible. Coat the new parts with heatproof grease, then reinstall the diverter valve and reassemble the faucet.

## How to Replace a Sprayer Hose

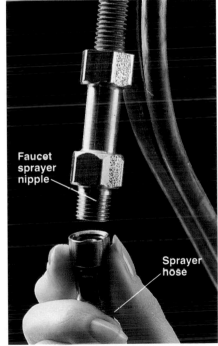

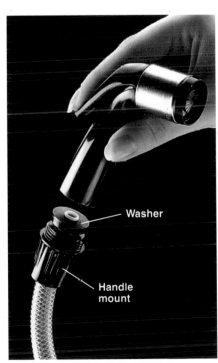

Faucet sprayer nipple

Sprayer hose

Washer

Handle mount

Retaining clip

Handle mount

**1** Unscrew sprayer hose from faucet sprayer nipple, using channel-type pliers. Pull sprayer hose through sink opening.

**2** Unscrew the sprayer head from the handle mount. Remove washer.

**3** Remove retainer clip with needlenose pliers, and discard old hose. Attach handle mount, retainer clip, washer, and sprayer head to new hose. Attach sprayer hose to faucet sprayer nipple on faucet.

Water line to shower head

Diverter valve

Hot water supply line

Cold water supply line

Diverter valve handle

# Fixing Three-handle Tub & Shower Faucets

A three-handle faucet type has handles to control hot and cold water, and a third handle that controls the diverter valve and directs water to either a tub spout or a shower head. The separate hot and cold handles indicate cartridge or compression faucet designs. To repair them, see pages 20 to 21 for cartridge, and 22 to 23 for compression.

If a diverter valve sticks, if water flow is weak, or if water runs out of the tub spout when the flow is directed to the shower head, the diverter needs to be repaired or replaced. Most diverter valves are similar to either compression or cartridge faucet valves. Compression type diverters can be repaired, but cartridge types should be replaced.

**Remember to turn off the water (page 8) before beginning work.**

### Everything You Need:

Tools: screwdriver, adjustable wrench or channel-type pliers, deep-set ratchet wrench, small wire brush.

Materials: replacement diverter cartridge or universal washer kit, heatproof grease, vinegar.

## How to Repair a Compression Diverter Valve

Escutcheon

Diverter valve handle

**1** Remove the diverter valve handle with a screwdriver. Unscrew or pry off the escutcheon.

**Bonnet nut**

**2** Remove bonnet nut with an adjustable wrench or channel-type pliers.

**3** Unscrew the stem assembly, using a deep-set ratchet wrench. If necessary, chip away any mortar surrounding the bonnet nut (page 29, step 2).

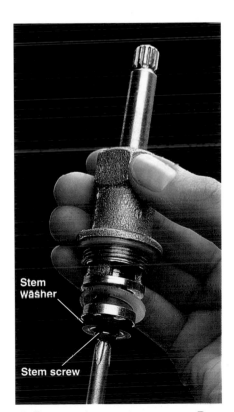

**Stem washer**

**Stem screw**

**4** Remove brass stem screw. Replace stem washer with an exact duplicate. If stem screw is worn, replace it.

**Retaining nut**

**Threaded spindle**

**5** Unscrew threaded spindle from retaining nut.

**6** Clean sediment and lime build-up from nut, using a small wire brush dipped in vinegar. Coat all parts with heatproof grease and reassemble diverter valve.

Water line to
shower head

Bonnet
nut

Valve stem

Cold water
supply line

Diverter lever

Hot water
supply line

Gate diverter

# Fixing Two-handle Tub & Shower Faucets

Two-handle tub and shower faucets are either cartridge or compression design. They may be repaired following the directions on pages 20 to 21 for cartridge, or pages 22 to 23 for compression. Because the valves of two-handle tub and shower faucets may be set inside the wall cavity, a deep-set socket wrench may be required to remove the valve stem.

Two-handle tub and shower designs have a gate diverter. A gate diverter is a simple mechanism located in the tub spout. A gate diverter closes the supply of water to the tub spout and redirects the flow to the shower head. Gate diverters seldom need repair. Occasionally, the lever may break, come loose, or refuse to stay in the UP position.

If the diverter fails to work properly, replace the tub spout. Tub spouts are inexpensive and easy to replace.

**Remember to turn off the water (page 8) before beginning work.**

### Everything You Need:

Tools: screwdriver, allen wrench, pipe wrench, channel-type pliers, small cold chisel, ball peen hammer, deep-set ratchet wrench.

Materials: masking tape or cloth, pipe joint compound, replacement faucet parts as needed.

## Tips on Replacing a Tub Spout

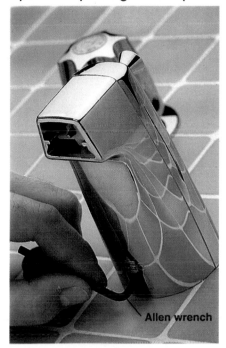

**Check underneath tub spout** for a small access slot. The slot indicates the spout is held in place with an allen screw. Remove the screw, using an allen wrench. Spout will slide off.

**Unscrew faucet spout.** Use a pipe wrench, or insert a large screwdriver or hammer handle into the spout opening and turn spout counterclockwise.

**Spread pipe joint compound** on threads of spout nipple before replacing spout.

## How to Remove a Deep-set Faucet Valve

**1** Remove handle, and unscrew the escutcheon with channel-type pliers. Pad the jaws of the pliers with masking tape to prevent scratching the escutcheon.

**2** Chip away any mortar surrounding the bonnet nut, using a ball peen hammer and a small cold chisel.

**3** Unscrew the bonnet nut with a deep-set ratchet wrench. Remove the bonnet nut and stem from the faucet body.

**Water supply line to shower head**

**Built-in shutoff valves**

**Control valve**

**Hot water supply line**

**Cold water supply line**

**Escutcheon**

**Gate diverter**

# Fixing Single-handle Tub & Shower Faucets

A single-handle tub and shower faucet has one valve that controls both water flow and temperature. Single-handle faucets may be ball-type, cartridge, or disc designs.

If a single-handle control valve leaks or does not function properly, disassemble the faucet, clean the valve, and replace any worn parts. Use the repair techniques described on page 13 for ball-type, or page 14 for disc-type. Repairing a single-handle sleeve cartridge faucet is shown on the opposite page.

Direction of the water flow to either the tub spout or the shower head is controlled by a gate diverter.

Gate diverters seldom need repair. Occasionally, the lever may break, come loose, or refuse to stay in the UP position. If the diverter fails to work properly, replace the tub spout (page 29).

### Everything You Need:

Tools: screwdriver, adjustable wrench, channel-type pliers.

Materials: replacement parts as needed.

## How to Repair a Single-handle Cartridge Tub & Shower Faucet

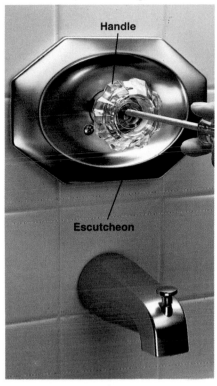

**1** Use a screwdriver to remove the handle and escutcheon.

**2** Turn off water supply at built-in shutoff valves or main shutoff valve (page 6).

**3** Unscrew and remove retaining ring or bonnet nut, using an adjustable wrench.

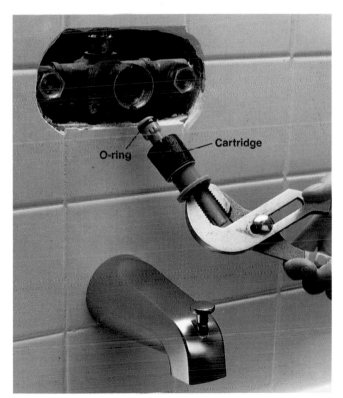

**4** Remove cartridge assembly by grasping end of valve with channel-type pliers and pulling gently.

**5** Flush valve body with clean water to remove sediment. Replace any worn O-rings. Reinstall cartridge and test valve. If faucet fails to work properly, replace the cartridge.

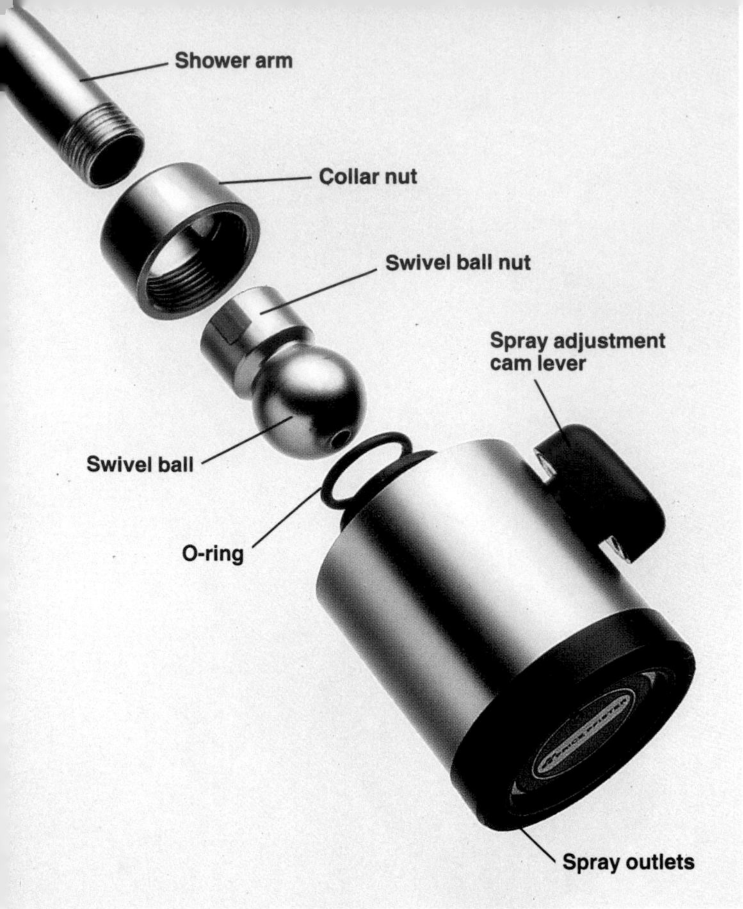

Labels on diagram:
- Shower arm
- Collar nut
- Swivel ball nut
- Spray adjustment cam lever
- Swivel ball
- O-ring
- Spray outlets

# Fixing & Replacing Shower Heads

If spray from the shower head is uneven, clean the spray holes. The outlet or inlet holes of the shower head may get clogged with mineral deposits.

Shower heads pivot into different positions. If a shower head does not stay in position, or if it leaks, replace the O-ring that seals against the swivel ball.

A tub can be equipped with a shower by installing a flexible shower adapter kit. Complete kits are available at hardware stores and home centers.

**A typical shower head** can be disassembled easily for cleaning and repair. Some shower heads include a spray adjustment cam lever that is used to change the force of the spray.

### Everything You Need:

Tools: adjustable wrench or channel-type pliers, pipe wrench, drill, glass & tile bit (if needed), mallet, screwdriver.

Materials: masking tape, thin wire (paper clip), heatproof grease, rag, replacement O-rings (if needed), masonry anchors, flexible shower adapter kit (optional).

## How to Clean & Repair a Shower Head

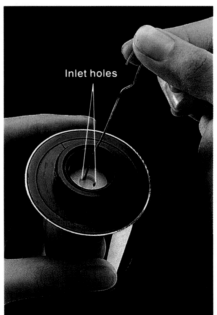

**1** Unscrew swivel ball nut, using an adjustable wrench or channel-type pliers. Wrap jaws of the tool with masking tape to prevent marring the finish. Unscrew collar nut from shower head.

**2** Clean outlet and inlet holes of shower head with a thin wire. Flush the head with clean water.

**3** Replace the O-ring, if necessary. Lubricate the O-ring with heatproof grease before installing.

# How to Install a Flexible Shower Adapter

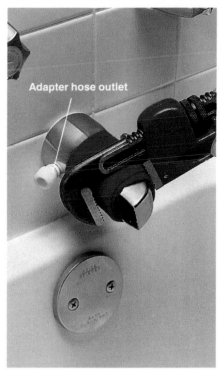

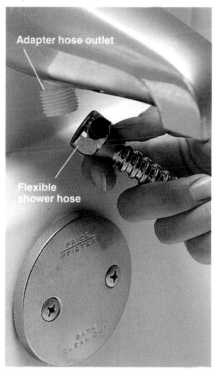

**1** Remove old tub spout (page 29). Install new tub spout from kit, using a pipe wrench. New spout will have an adapter hose outlet. Wrap the tub spout with a rag to prevent damage to the chrome finish.

**2** Attach flexible shower hose to the adaptor hose outlet. Tighten with an adjustable wrench or channel-type pliers.

**3** Determine location of shower head hanger. Use hose length as a guide, and make sure shower head can be easily lifted off hanger.

**4** Mark hole locations. Use a glass and tile bit to drill holes in ceramic tile for masonry anchors.

**5** Insert anchors into holes, and tap into place with a wooden or rubber mallet.

**6** Fasten shower head holder to the wall, and hang shower head.

Shutoff valve

Globe valve

Gate valve

Saddle valve

Hose bib

# Repairing Valves & Hose Bibs

Valves make it possible to shut off water at any point in the supply system. If a pipe breaks or a plumbing fixture begins to leak, you can shut off water to the damaged area so it can be repaired. A hose bib is a faucet with a threaded spout, often used to connect utility or appliance hoses.

Valves and hose bibs leak when washers or seals wear out. Replacement parts can be found in the same universal washer kits used to repair compression faucets (page 22). Coat replacement washers with heatproof grease to keep them soft and prevent cracking.

**Remember to turn off the water before beginning work (page 6).**

### Everything You Need:

Tools: screwdriver, adjustable wrench.

Materials: universal washer kit, heatproof grease.

## How to Fix a Leaky Hose Bib

Packing nut

**1** Remove the handle screw, and lift off the handle. Unscrew the packing nut with an adjustable wrench.

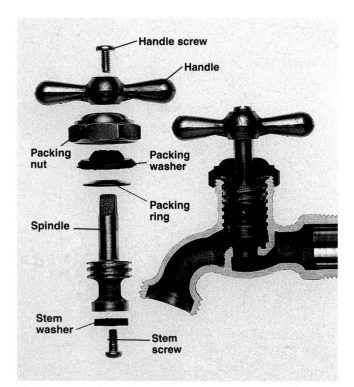

Handle screw

Handle

Packing nut

Packing washer

Packing ring

Spindle

Stem washer

Stem screw

**2** Unscrew the spindle from the valve body. Remove the stem screw and replace the stem washer. Replace the packing washer, and reassemble the valve.

# Common Types of Valves

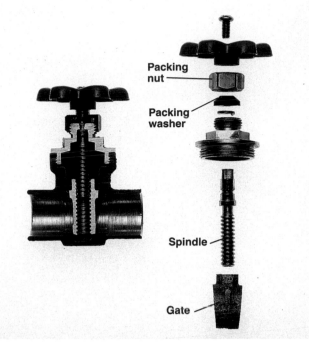

**Gate valve** has a movable brass wedge, or "gate," that screws up and down to control water flow. Gate valves may develop leaks around the handle. Repair leaks by replacing the packing washer or packing string found underneath the packing nut.

**Globe valve** has a curved chamber. Repair leaks around the handle by replacing the packing washer. If valve does not fully stop water flow when closed, replace the stem washer.

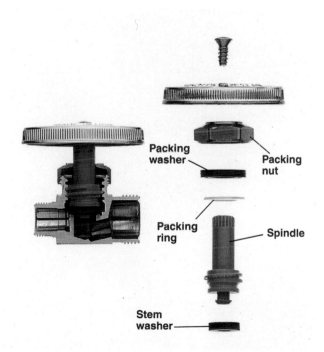

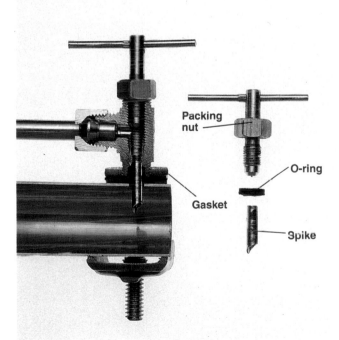

**Shutoff valve** controls water supply to a single fixture (pages 22 to 23). Shutoff valve has a plastic spindle with a packing washer and a snap-on stem washer. Repair leaks around the handle by replacing the packing washer. If valve does not fully stop water flow when closed, replace the stem washer.

**Saddle valve** is a small fitting often used to connect a refrigerator icemaker or sink-mounted water filter to a copper water pipe. Saddle valve contains a hollow metal spike that punctures water pipe when valve is first closed. Fitting is sealed with a rubber gasket. Repair leaks around the handle by replacing the O-ring under the packing nut.

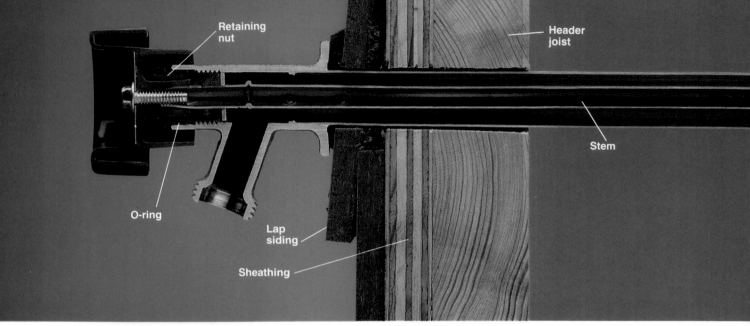

Labels on image: Retaining nut, Header joist, Stem, O-ring, Lap siding, Sheathing

**Frost-proof sillcock** is mounted against the header joist (sill), and has a long stem that reaches 6" to 30" inside the house to protect the valve from cold. A sillcock should angle downward slightly to provide drainage. The stem washer and O-ring (or packing string) can be replaced if the sillcock begins to leak. In a copper plumbing system,

# Installing & Repairing Sillcocks

A sillcock is a compression faucet attached to the outside of the house. Repair a leaky sillcock by replacing the stem washer and the O-ring.

Sillcocks can be damaged by frost. To repair a pipe that has ruptured due to frost, see pages 70 to 71. To prevent pipes from rupturing, close the indoor shutoff valves at the start of the cold weather season, disconnect all garden hoses, and open the sillcock to let trapped water drain out.

A special frost-proof sillcock has a long stem that reaches at least 6" inside the house to protect it from cold. Install a sillcock so the pipe angles downward from the shutoff valve. This allows water to drain away each time the faucet is turned off.

**Remember to turn off the water before beginning work (page 6).**

**Everything You Need:**

Tools: screwdriver, channel-type pliers, pencil, right-angle drill or standard drill, 1" spade bit, caulk gun, hacksaw or tubing cutter, propane torch.

Materials: universal washer kit, sillcock, silicone caulk, 2" corrosion-resistant screws, copper pipe, T-fitting, Teflon™ tape, threaded adapter, shutoff valve, emery cloth, soldering paste (flux), solder.

## How to Repair a Sillcock

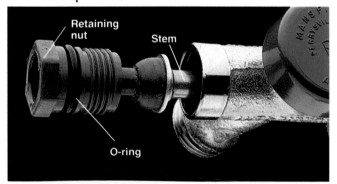

Labels on image: Retaining nut, Stem, O-ring

**1** Remove sillcock handle, and loosen retaining nut with channel-type pliers. Remove stem. Replace O-ring found on retaining nut or stem.

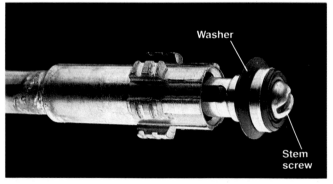

Labels on image: Washer, Stem screw

**2** Remove the brass stem screw at the end of the stem, and replace the washer. Reassemble the sillcock.

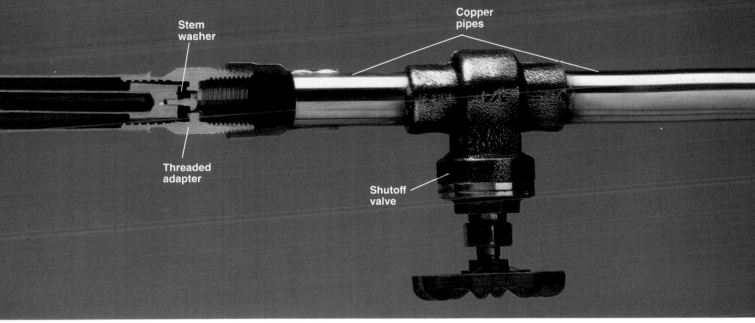

the sillcock is connected to a nearby cold water supply pipe with a threaded adapter, two lengths of soldered copper pipe, and a shutoff valve. A T-fitting (not shown) is used to tap into an existing cold water pipe.

## How to Install a Frost-proof Sillcock

**1** Locate position of hole for sillcock. From nearest cold water pipe, mark a point on header joist that is slightly lower than water pipe. Drill a hole through header, sheathing, and siding, using a 1" spade bit.

**2** Apply a thick bead of silicone caulk to bottom of sillcock flange, then insert sillcock into hole, and attach to siding with 2" corrosion-resistant screws. Turn handle to ON position. Wipe away excess caulk.

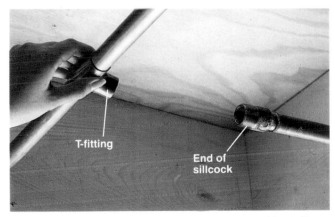

**3** Mark cold water pipe, then cut pipe and install a T-fitting. Wrap Teflon™ tape around threads of sillcock.

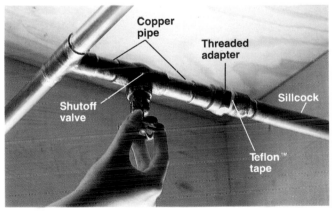

**4** Join T-fitting to sillcock with a threaded adapter, a shutoff valve, and two lengths of copper pipe. Prepare pipes and solder the joints. Turn on water, and close sillcock when water runs steadily.

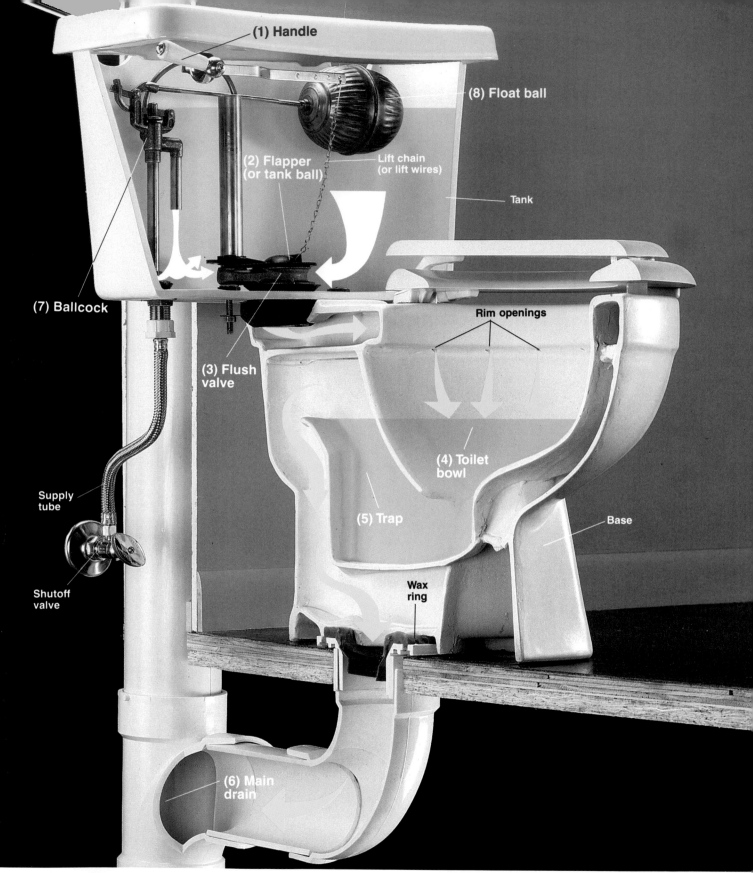

**(1) Handle**

**(8) Float ball**

**(2) Flapper (or tank ball)**

**Lift chain (or lift wires)**

**Tank**

**(7) Ballcock**

**Rim openings**

**(3) Flush valve**

**Supply tube**

**(4) Toilet bowl**

**(5) Trap**

**Base**

**Shutoff valve**

**Wax ring**

**(6) Main drain**

**How a toilet works:** When the **handle (1)** is pushed, the lift chain raises a rubber seal, called a **flapper or tank ball (2)**. Water in the tank rushes down through the **flush valve opening (3)** in the bottom of the tank, into the **toilet bowl (4)**. Waste water in the bowl is forced through the **trap (5)** into the **main drain (6)**.

When the toilet tank is empty, the flapper seals the tank, and a water supply valve, called a **ballcock (7)**, refills the toilet tank. The ballcock is controlled by a **float ball (8)** that rides on the surface of the water. When the tank is full, the float ball automatically shuts off the ballcock.

# Common Toilet Problems

A clogged toilet is one of the most common plumbing problems. If a toilet overflows or flushes sluggishly, clear the clog with a plunger or closet auger (page 54). If the problem persists, the clog may be in the main waste and vent stack (page 61).

Most other toilet problems are fixed easily with minor adjustments that require no disassembly or replacement parts. You can make these adjustments in a few minutes, using simple tools (page 40).

If minor adjustments do not fix the problem, further repairs will be needed. The parts of a standard toilet are not difficult to take apart, and most repair projects can be completed in less than an hour.

A recurring puddle of water on the floor around a toilet may be caused by a crack in the toilet base or in the tank. A damaged toilet should be replaced. Installing a new toilet is an easy project that can be finished in three or four hours.

A standard two-piece toilet has an upper tank that is bolted to a base. This type of toilet uses a simple gravity-operated flush system, and can be repaired easily using the directions on the following pages. Some one-piece toilets use a complicated, high-pressure flush valve. Repairing these toilets can be difficult, so this work should be left to a professional.

| Problems | Repairs |
| --- | --- |
| Toilet handle sticks, or is hard to push. | 1. Adjust lift wires (page 40). <br> 2. Clean & adjust handle (page 40). |
| Handle is loose. | 1. Adjust handle (page 40). <br> 2. Reattach lift chain or lift wires to lever (page 40). |
| Toilet will not flush at all. | 1. Make sure water is turned on. <br> 2. Adjust lift chain or lift wires (page 40). |
| Toilet does not flush completely. | 1. Adjust lift chain (page 40). <br> 2. Adjust water level in tank (page 42). |
| Toilet overflows, or flushes sluggishly. | 1. Clear clogged toilet (page 54). <br> 2. Clear clogged main waste and vent stack (page 61). |
| Toilet runs continuously. | 1. Adjust lift wires or lift chain (page 40). <br> 2. Replace leaky float ball (page 41). <br> 3. Adjust water level in tank (page 42) <br> 4. Adjust & clean flush valve (page 45). <br> 5. Replace flush valve (page 45). <br> 6. Repair or replace ballcock (pages 43 to 44). |
| Water on floor around toilet. | 1. Tighten tank bolts and water connections (page 46). <br> 2. Insulate tank to prevent condensation (page 46). <br> 3. Replace wax ring (pages 47 to 48). <br> 4. Replace cracked tank or bowl (pages 46 to 49) |

# Making Minor Adjustments

Many common toilet problems can be fixed by making minor adjustments to the handle and the attached lift chain (or lift wires).

If the handle sticks or is hard to push, remove the tank cover and clean the handle mounting nut. Make sure the lift wires are straight.

If the toilet will not flush completely unless the handle is held down, you may need to remove excess slack in the lift chain.

If the toilet will not flush at all, the lift chain may be broken or may need to be reattached to the handle lever.

A continuously running toilet (page opposite) can be caused by bent lift wires, kinks in a lift chain, or lime buildup on the handle mounting nut. Clean and adjust the handle and the lift wires or chain to fix the problem.

**Everything You Need:**

Tools: adjustable wrench, needlenose pliers, screwdriver, small wire brush.

Materials: vinegar.

## How to Adjust a Toilet Handle & Lift Chain (or Lift Wires)

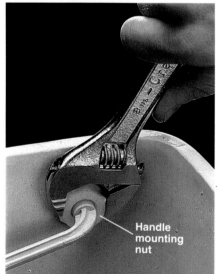

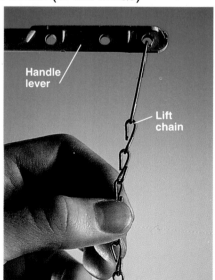

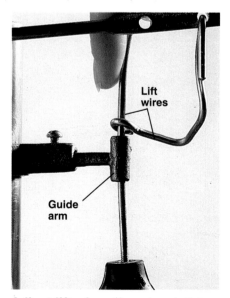

**Clean and adjust handle** mounting nut so handle operates smoothly. Mounting nut has reversed threads. Loosen nut by turning clockwise; tighten by turning counterclockwise. Remove lime buildup by scrubbing handle parts with a brush dipped in vinegar.

**Adjust lift chain** so it hangs straight from handle lever, with about ½" of slack. Remove excess slack in chain by hooking the chain in a different hole in the handle lever, or by removing links with needlenose pliers. A broken lift chain must be replaced.

**Adjust lift wires** (found on toilets without lift chains) so that wires are straight and operate smoothly when handle is pushed. A sticky handle often can be fixed by straightening bent lift wires.

# Fixing a Running Toilet

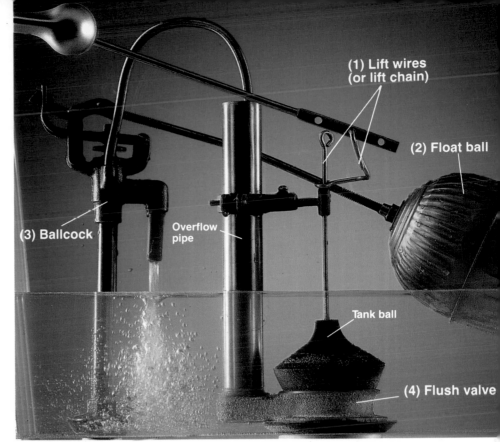

The sound of continuously running water occurs if fresh water continues to enter the toilet tank after the flush cycle is complete. A running toilet can waste 20 or more gallons of fresh water each day.

To fix a running toilet, first jiggle the toilet handle. If the sound of running water stops, then either the handle or the lift wires (or lift chain) need to be adjusted (page opposite).

If the sound of running water does not stop when the handle is jiggled, then remove the tank cover and check to see if the float ball is touching the side of the tank. If necessary, bend the float arm to reposition the float ball away from the side of the tank. Make sure the float ball is not leaking. To check for leaks, unscrew the float ball and shake it gently. If there is water inside the ball, replace it.

If these minor adjustments do not fix the problem, then you will need to adjust or repair the ballcock or the flush valve (photo, right). Follow the directions on the following pages.

### Everything You Need:

Tools: screwdriver, small wire brush, sponge, adjustable wrenches, spud wrench or channel-type pliers.

Materials: universal washer kit, ballcock (if needed), ballcock seals, emery cloth, Scotch Brite® pad, flapper or tank ball, flush valve (if needed).

**(1) Lift wires (or lift chain)**
**(2) Float ball**
**(3) Ballcock**
**Overflow pipe**
**Tank ball**
**(4) Flush valve**

**The sound of continuously running water** can be caused by several different problems: if the **lift wire (1)** (or lift chain) is bent or kinked; if the **float ball (2)** leaks or rubs against the side of the tank; if a faulty **ballcock (3)** does not shut off the fresh water supply; or if the **flush valve (4)** allows water to leak down into the toilet bowl. First, check the lift wires and float ball. If making simple adjustments and repairs to these parts does not fix the problem, then you will need to repair the ballcock or flush valve (photo, below).

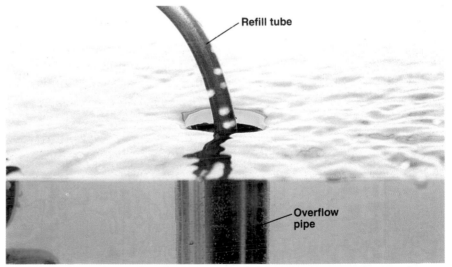

**Refill tube**

**Overflow pipe**

**Check the overflow pipe** if the sound of running water continues after the float ball and lift wires are adjusted. If you see **water flowing into the overflow pipe**, the ballcock needs to be repaired. First, adjust ballcock to lower the water level in the tank (page 42). If problem continues, repair or replace the ballcock (pages 43 to 44). If **water is not flowing into the overflow pipe**, then the flush valve needs to be repaired (page 45). First check the tank ball (or flapper) for wear, and replace if necessary. If problem continues, replace the flush valve.

# How to Adjust a Ballcock to Set Water Level

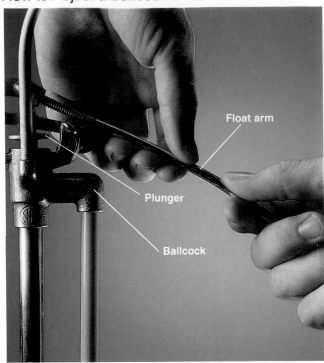

**Traditional plunger-valve ballcock** is made of brass. Water flow is controlled by a plunger attached to the float arm and ball. Lower the water level by bending the float arm downward slightly. Raise the water level by bending float arm upward.

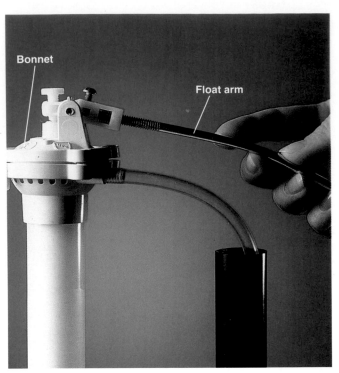

**Diaphragm ballcock** usually is made of plastic, and has a wide bonnet that contains a rubber diaphragm. Lower the water level by bending the float arm downward slightly. Raise the water level by bending float arm upward.

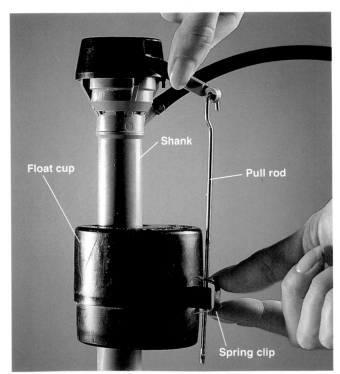

**Float cup ballcock** is made of plastic, and is easy to adjust. Lower the water level by pinching spring clip on pull rod, and moving float cup downward on the ballcock shank. Raise the water level by moving the cup upward.

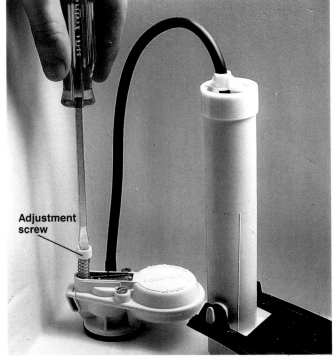

**Floatless ballcock** controls water level with a pressure-sensing device. Lower the water level by turning the adjustment screw counterclockwise, ½ turn at a time. Raise water level by turning screw clockwise. Floatless ballcocks are repair-free, but eventually may need to be replaced.

## How to Repair a Plunger-valve Ballcock

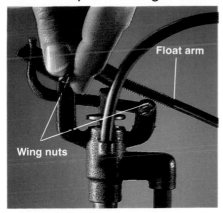

**1** Shut off the water, and flush to empty the tank. Remove the wing nuts on the ballcock. Slip out the float arm.

**2** Pull up on plunger to remove it. Pry out packing washer or O-ring. Pry out plunger washer. (Remove stem screw, if necessary.)

**3** Install replacement washers. Clean sediment from inside of ballcock with a wire brush. Re-assemble ballcock.

## How to Repair a Diaphragm Ballcock

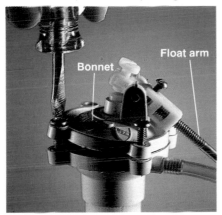

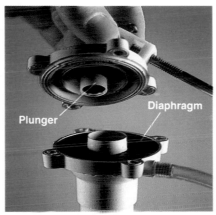

**1** Shut off the water, and flush to empty the tank. Remove the screws from the bonnet.

**2** Lift off float arm with bonnet attached. Check diaphragm and plunger for wear.

**3** Replace any stiff or cracked parts. If assembly is badly worn, replace the entire ballcock (page 44).

## How to Repair a Float Cup Ballcock

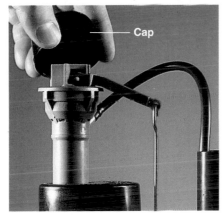

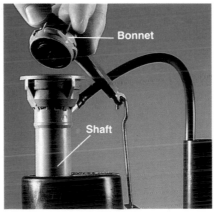

**1** Shut off the water, and flush to empty the tank. Remove the ballcock cap.

**2** Remove bonnet by pushing down on shaft and turning counterclockwise. Clean out sediment inside ballcock with wire brush.

**3** Replace the seal. If assembly is badly worn, replace the entire ballcock (page 44).

## How to Install a New Ballcock

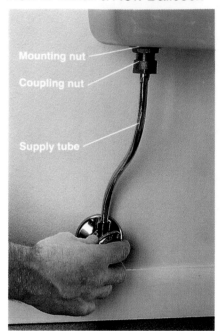

**1** Shut off water, and flush toilet to empty tank. Use a sponge to remove remaining water. Disconnect supply tube coupling nut and ballcock mounting nut with adjustable wrench. Remove old ballcock.

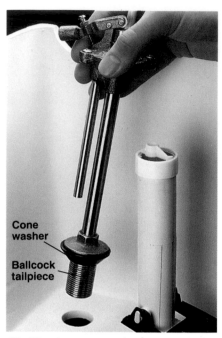

**2** Attach cone washer to new ballcock tailpiece and insert tailpiece into tank opening.

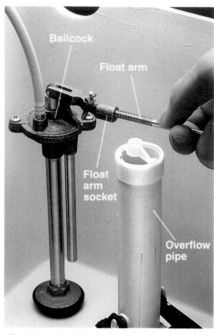

**3** Align the float arm socket so that float arm will pass behind overflow pipe. Screw float arm onto ballcock. Screw float ball onto float arm.

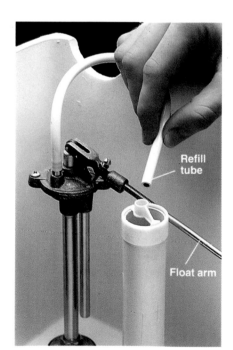

**4** Bend or clip refill tube so tip is inside overflow pipe.

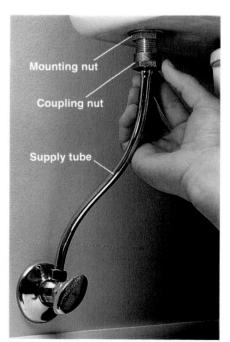

**5** Screw mounting nut and supply tube coupling nut onto ballcock tailpiece, and tighten with an adjustable wrench. Turn on the water, and check for leaks.

**6** Adjust the water level in the tank so it is about ½" below top of the overflow pipe (page 42).

## How to Adjust & Clean a Flush Valve

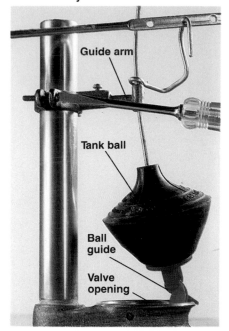

**Adjust tank ball (or flapper)** so it is directly over flush valve. Tank ball has a guide arm that can be loosened so that tank ball can be repositioned. (Some tank balls have a ball guide that helps seat the tank ball into the flush valve.)

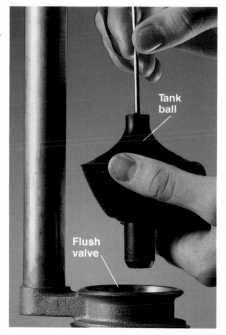

**Replace the tank ball** if it is cracked or worn. Tank balls have a threaded fitting that screws onto the lift wire. Clean opening of the flush valve, using emery cloth (for brass valves) or a Scotch Brite® pad (for plastic valves).

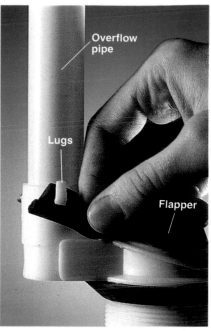

**Replace flapper** if it is worn. Flappers are attached to small lugs on the sides of overflow pipe.

## How to Install a New Flush Valve

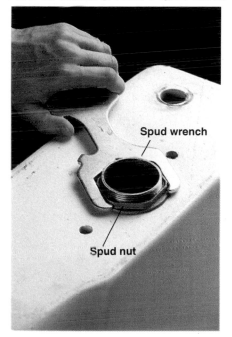

**1** Shut off water, disconnect ball-cock (page opposite, step 1), and remove toilet tank (page 47, steps 1 and 2). Remove old flush valve by unscrewing spud nut with spud wrench or channel-type pliers.

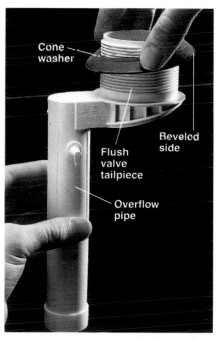

**2** Slide cone washer onto tailpiece of new flush valve. Beveled side of cone washer should face end of tailpiece. Insert flush valve into tank opening so that overflow pipe faces ballcock.

**3** Screw spud nut onto tailpiece of flush valve, and tighten with a spud wrench or channel-type pliers. Place soft spud washer over tailpiece, and reinstall toilet tank (pages 48 to 49).

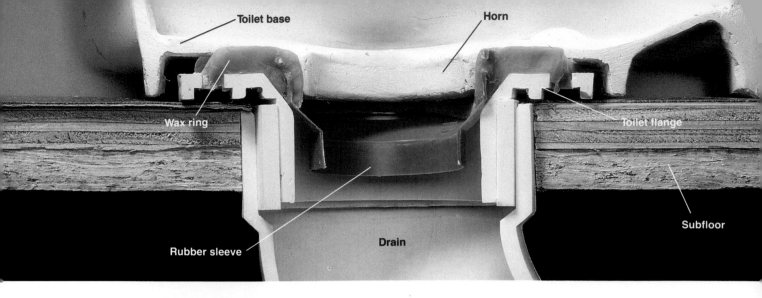

Toilet base · Horn · Wax ring · Toilet flange · Rubber sleeve · Drain · Subfloor

# Fixing a Leaking Toilet

Water leaking onto the floor around a toilet may be caused by several different problems. The leaking must be fixed as soon as possible to prevent moisture from damaging the subfloor.

First, make sure all connections are tight. If moisture drips from the tank during humid weather, it is probably condensation. Fix this "sweating" problem by insulating the inside of the tank with foam panels. A crack in a toilet tank also can cause leaks. A cracked tank must be replaced.

Water seeping around the base of a toilet can be caused by an old wax ring that no longer seals against the drain (photo, above), or by a cracked toilet base. If leaking occurs during or just after a flush, replace the wax ring. If leaking is constant, the toilet base is cracked and must be replaced.

New toilets sometimes are sold with flush valves and ballcocks already installed. If these parts are not included, you will need to purchase them. When buying a new toilet, consider a water-saver design. Water-saver toilets use less than half the water needed by a standard toilet.

### Everything You Need:

Tools: sponge, adjustable wrench, putty knife, ratchet wrench, screwdriver.

Materials: tank liner kit, abrasive cleanser, rag, wax ring, plumber's putty. *For new installation:* new toilet, toilet handle, ballcock, flush valve, tank bolts, toilet seat.

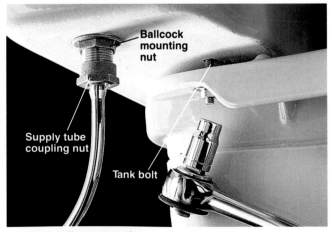

Ballcock mounting nut · Supply tube coupling nut · Tank bolt

**Tighten all connections** slightly. Tighten nuts on tank bolts with a ratchet wrench. Tighten ballcock mounting nut and supply tube coupling nut with an adjustable wrench. **Caution: overtightening tank bolts may crack the toilet tank.**

**Insulate toilet tank** to prevent "sweating," using a toilet liner kit. First, shut off water, drain tank, and clean inside of tank with abrasive cleanser. Cut plastic foam panels to fit bottom, sides, front, and back of tank. Attach panels to tank with adhesive (included in kit). Let adhesive cure as directed.

# How to Remove & Replace a Wax Ring & Toilet

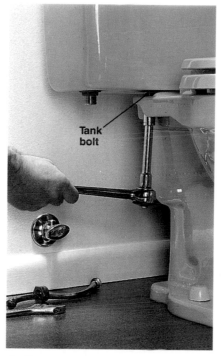

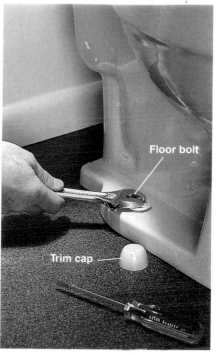

**1** Turn off water, and flush to empty toilet tank. Use a sponge to remove remaining water in tank and bowl. Disconnect supply tube with an adjustable wrench.

**2** Remove the nuts from the tank bolts with a ratchet wrench. Carefully remove the tank and set it aside.

**3** Pry off the floor bolt trim caps at the base of the toilet. Remove the floor nuts with an adjustable wrench.

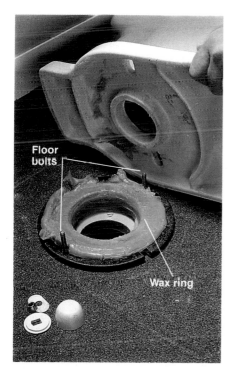

**4** Straddle the toilet and rock the bowl from side to side until the seal breaks. Carefully lift the toilet off the floor bolts and set it on its side. Small amount of water may spill from the toilet trap.

**5** Remove old wax from the toilet flange in the floor. Plug the drain opening with a damp rag to prevent sewer gases from rising into the house.

**6** If old toilet will be reused, clean old wax and putty from the horn and the base of the toilet.

(continued next page)

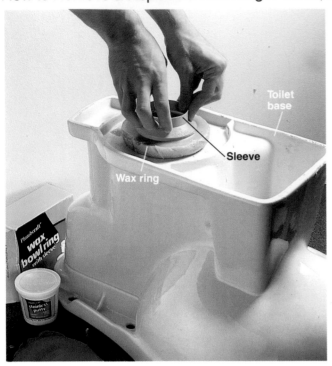

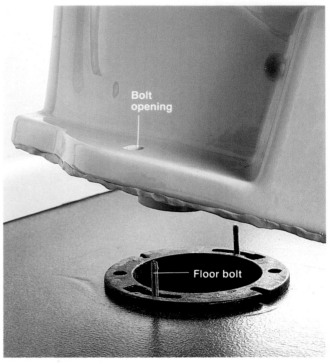

**7** Turn stool upside down. Place new wax ring over drain horn. If ring has a rubber or plastic sleeve, sleeve should face away from toilet. Apply a bead of plumber's putty to bottom edge of toilet base.

**8** Position the toilet over drain so that the floor bolts fit through openings in base of toilet. Thread washers and nuts onto floor bolts, and tighten with adjustable wrench until snug.

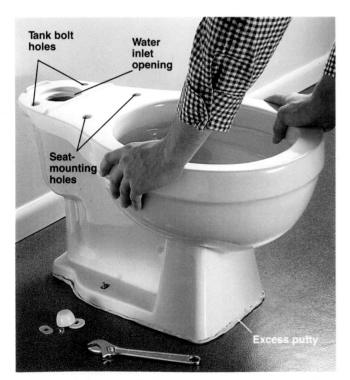

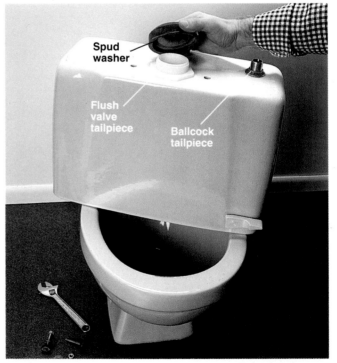

**9** Press down on toilet base to compress wax and putty. Retighten floor nuts until snug. **Caution: over-tightening nuts may crack the base.** Wipe away excess plumber's putty. Cover nuts with trim caps.

**10** Prepare tank for installation. If necessary, install a handle (page 40), ballcock (page 44), and flush valve (page 45). Carefully turn tank upside down, and place soft spud washer over the flush valve tailpiece.

**11** Turn tank right side up and position it on rear of toilet base so that spud washer is centered in water inlet opening.

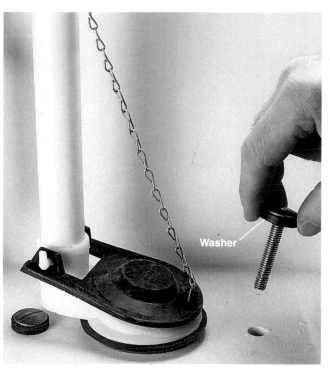

Washer

**12** Line up the tank bolt holes with holes in base of toilet. Slide rubber washers onto the tank bolts and place the bolts through holes. From underneath the tank, thread washers and nuts onto the bolts.

**13** Tighten nuts with ratchet wrench until tank is snug. Use caution when tightening nuts: most toilet tanks rest on the spud washer, not directly on the toilet base.

**14** Attach the water supply tube to the ballcock tailpiece with an adjustable wrench (page 44). Turn on the water and test toilet. Tighten tank bolts and water connections, if necessary.

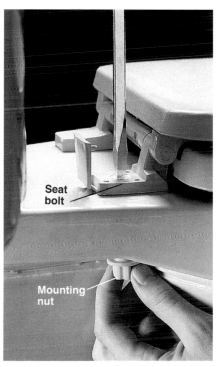

Seat bolt

Mounting nut

**15** Position the new toilet seat, if needed, inserting seat bolts into mounting holes in toilet. Screw mounting nuts onto the seat bolts, and tighten.

# Clearing Clogs & Fixing Drains

Clear a clogged drain with a plunger, hand auger, or blow bag. A plunger breaks up clogs by forcing air pressure into the drain line. Because a plunger is effective and simple to use, it should be the first choice for clearing a clog.

A hand auger has a flexible steel cable that is pushed into the drain line to break up or remove obstructions. An auger is easy to use, but for best results the user must know the "feel" of the cable in the drain line. A little experience often is necessary to tell the difference between a soap clog and a bend in the drain line (pages 62 to 63).

A blow bag hooks to a garden hose and uses water pressure to clear clogs. Blow bags are most effective on clogs in floor drains (page 59).

Use caustic, acid-based chemical drain cleaners only as a last resort. These drain cleaners, usually available at hardware stores and supermarkets, will dissolve clogs, but they also may damage pipes and must be handled with caution. Always read the manufacturer's directions completely.

Regular maintenance helps keep drains working properly. Flush drains once each week with hot tap water to keep them free of soap, grease, and debris. Or, treat drains once every six months with a non-caustic (copper sulfide- or sodium hydroxide-based) drain cleaner. A non-caustic cleaner will not harm pipes.

Occasionally, leaks may occur in the drain lines or around the drain opening. Most leaks in drain lines are fixed easily by gently tightening all pipe connections. If the leak is at the sink drain opening, fix or replace the strainer body assembly (page 53).

# Clearing Clogged Sinks

Every sink has a drain trap and a fixture drain line. Sink clogs usually are caused by a buildup of soap and hair in the trap or fixture drain line. Remove clogs by using a plunger, disconnecting and cleaning the trap (page 52), or using a hand auger (pages 62 to 63).

Many sinks hold water with a mechanical plug called a *pop-up stopper*. If the sink will not hold standing water, or if water in the sink drains too slowly, the pop-up stopper must be cleaned and adjusted (page 52).

### Everything You Need:

Tools: plunger, channel-type pliers, small wire brush, screwdriver.

Materials: rag, bucket, replacement gaskets.

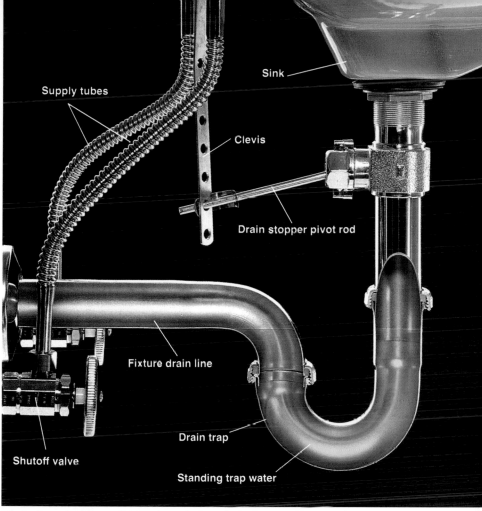

**Drain trap holds water** that seals the drain line and prevents sewer gases from entering the home. Each time a drain is used, the standing trap water is flushed away and replaced by new water. The shape of the trap and fixture drain line may resemble the letter "P," and sink traps sometimes are called P-traps.

## How to Clear Sink Drains with a Plunger

**1** Remove drain stopper. Some pop-up stoppers lift out directly; others turn counterclockwise. On some older types of stoppers, the pivot rod must be removed to free the stopper.

**2** Stuff a wet rag in sink overflow opening. Rag prevents air from breaking the suction of the plunger. Place plunger cup over drain and run enough water to cover the rubber cup. Move plunger handle up and down rapidly to break up the clog.

## How to Clean & Adjust a Pop-up Sink Drain Stopper

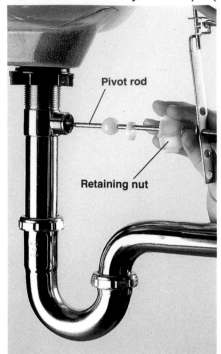

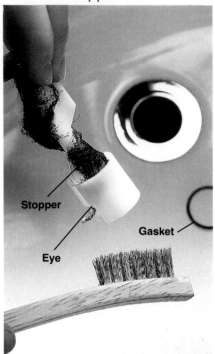

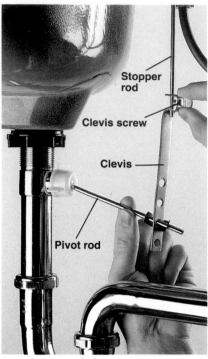

**1** Raise stopper lever to full up-right (closed) position. Unscrew the retaining nut that holds pivot rod in position. Pull pivot rod out of drain pipe to release stopper.

**2** Remove stopper. Clean debris from stopper, using a small wire brush. Inspect gasket for wear or damage, and replace if necessary. Reinstall stopper.

**3** If sink does not drain properly, adjust clevis. Loosen clevis screw. Slide clevis up or down on stopper rod to adjust position of stopper. Tighten clevis screw.

## How to Remove & Clean a Sink Drain Trap

**1** Place bucket under trap to catch water and debris. Loosen slip nuts on trap bend with channel-type pliers. Unscrew nuts by hand and slide away from connections. Pull off trap bend.

**2** Dump out debris. Clean trap bend with a small wire brush. Inspect slip nut washers for wear, and replace if necessary. Reinstall trap bend, and tighten slip nuts.

# Fixing Leaky Sink Strainers

A leak under a sink may be caused by a strainer body that is not properly sealed to the sink drain opening. To check for leaks, close the drain stopper and fill sink with water. From underneath sink, inspect the strainer assembly for leaks.

Remove the strainer body, clean it, and replace the gaskets and plumber's putty. Or, replace the strainer with a new one, available at home centers.

## Everything You Need:

Tools: channel-type pliers, spud wrench, hammer, putty knife.

Materials: plumber's putty, replacement parts (if needed).

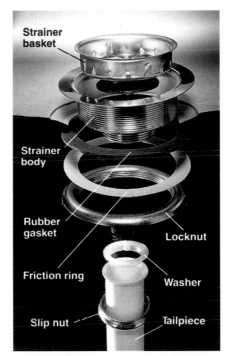

**Sink strainer assembly** connects the sink to the drain line. Leaks may occur where the strainer body seals against the lip of the drain opening.

**1** Unscrew slip nuts from both ends of tailpiece, using channel-type pliers. Disconnect tailpiece from strainer body and trap bend. Remove tailpiece.

**2** Remove the locknut, using a spud wrench. Stubborn locknuts may be removed by tapping on the lugs with a hammer. Unscrew the locknut completely, and remove the strainer assembly.

**3** Remove old putty from the drain opening, using a putty knife. If reusing the old strainer body, clean off old putty from under the flange. Old gaskets and washers should be replaced.

**4** Apply a bead of plumber's putty to the lip of the drain opening. Press strainer body into drain opening. From under the sink, place rubber gasket, then metal or fiber friction ring, over strainer. Reinstall locknut and tighten. Reinstall tailpiece.

# Clearing Clogged Toilets

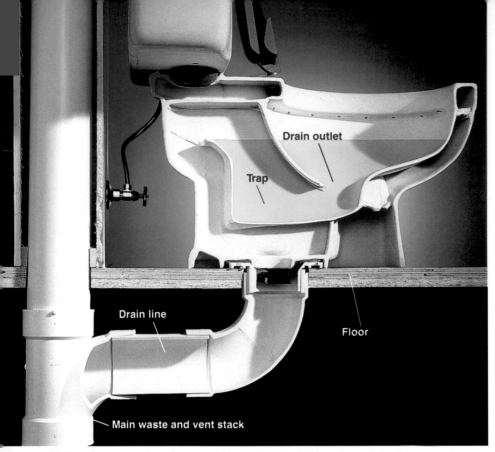

Most toilet clogs occur because an object is stuck inside the toilet trap. Use a flanged plunger or a closet auger to remove the clog.

A toilet that is sluggish during the flush cycle may be partially blocked. Clear the blockage with a plunger or closet auger. Occasionally, a sluggish toilet flush indicates a blocked waste and vent stack. Clear the stack as shown on page 61.

**Toilet drain system** has a drain outlet at the bottom of the bowl and a built-in trap. The toilet drain is connected to a drain line and a main waste and vent stack.

**Everything You Need:**

Tools: flanged plunger, closet auger.

Materials: bucket.

## How to Clear a Toilet with a Plunger

**Place cup of flanged plunger** over drain outlet opening. Plunge up and down rapidly. Slowly pour a bucket of water into bowl to flush debris through drain. If toilet does not drain, repeat plunging, or clear clog with a closet auger.

## How to Clear a Toilet with a Closet Auger

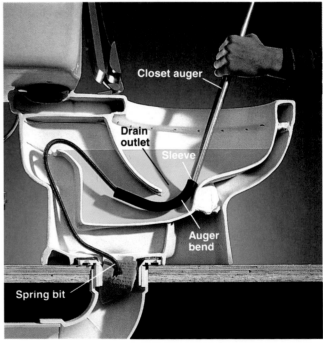

**Place the auger bend** in the bottom of the drain opening, and push the auger cable into the trap. Crank the auger handle in a clockwise direction to snag obstruction. Continue cranking while retrieving the cable to pull the obstruction out of the trap.

# Clearing Clogged Shower Drains

Shower drain clogs usually are caused by an accumulation of hair in the drain line. Remove the strainer cover and look for clogs in the drain opening (below). Some clogs are removed easily with a piece of stiff wire.

Stubborn clogs should be removed with a plunger or hand auger.

### Everything You Need:

Tools: screwdriver, flashlight, plunger, hand auger.

Materials: stiff wire.

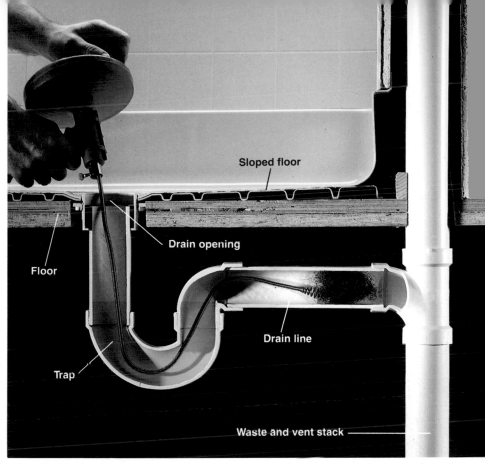

**Shower drain system** has a sloped floor, a drain opening, a trap, and a drain line that connects to a branch drain line or waste and vent stack.

## How to Clear a Shower Drain

**Check for clogs.** Remove strainer cover, using a screwdriver. Use a flashlight to look for hair clogs in the drain opening. Use a stiff wire to clear shower drain of hair or to snag any obstructions.

**Use a plunger** to clear most shower drain clogs. Place the rubber cup over the drain opening. Pour enough water into the shower stall to cover the lip of the cup. Move plunger handle up and down rapidly.

**Clear stubborn clogs** in the shower drain with a hand auger. Use the auger as shown on pages 62 to 63.

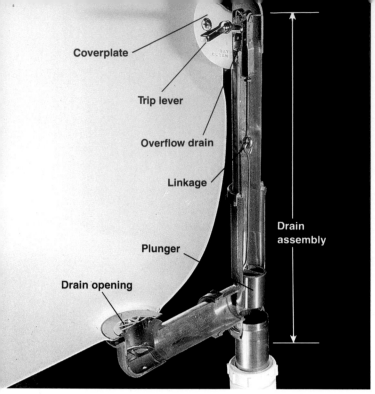

Plunger-type tub drain has a hollow brass plug, called a *plunger*, that slides up and down inside the overflow drain to seal off the water flow. The plunger is moved by a trip lever and linkage that runs through the overflow drain.

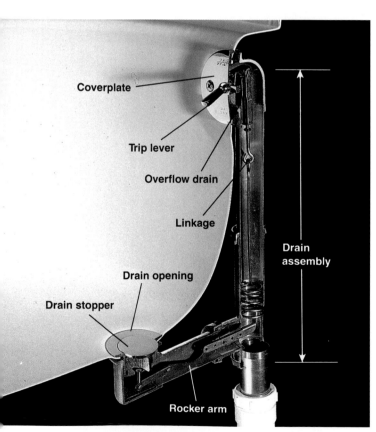

Pop-up tub drain has a rocker arm that pivots to open or close a metal drain stopper. The rocker arm is moved by a trip lever and linkage that runs through the overflow drain.

# Fixing Tub Drains

When water in the tub drains slowly or not at all, remove and inspect the drain assembly. Both plunger and pop-up type drain mechanisms catch hair and other debris that cause clogs.

If cleaning the drain assembly does not fix the problem, the tub drain line is clogged. Clear the line with a plunger or a hand auger. Always stuff a wet rag in the overflow drain opening before plunging the tub drain. The rag prevents air from breaking the suction of the plunger. When using an auger, always insert the cable down through the overflow drain opening.

If the tub will not hold water with the drain closed, or if the tub continues to drain slowly after the assembly has been cleaned, then the drain assembly needs adjustment. Remove the assembly, and follow the instructions on the opposite page.

## Everything You Need:

Tools: plunger, screwdriver, small wire brush, needlenose pliers, hand auger.

Materials: vinegar, heatproof grease, rag.

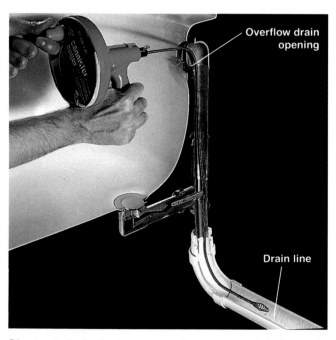

Clear a tub drain by running the auger cable through the overflow opening. First, remove the coverplate and carefully lift out the drain linkage (page opposite). Push auger cable into the opening until resistance is felt (pages 62 to 63). After using the auger, replace drain linkage. Open drain and run hot water through drain to flush out any debris.

## How to Clean & Adjust a Plunger-type Tub Drain

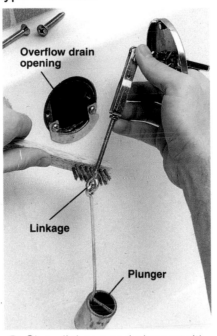

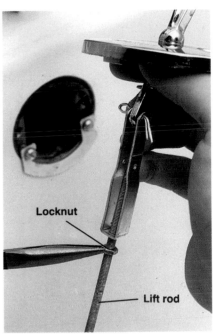

**1** Remove screws on coverplate. Carefully pull coverplate, linkage, and plunger from the overflow drain opening.

**2** Clean linkage and plunger with a small wire brush dipped in vinegar. Lubricate assembly with heatproof grease.

**3** Adjust drain flow and fix leaks by adjusting linkage. Unscrew locknut on threaded lift rod, using needlenose pliers. Screw rod down about 1/8". Tighten locknut and reinstall entire assembly.

## How to Clean & Adjust a Pop-up Tub Drain

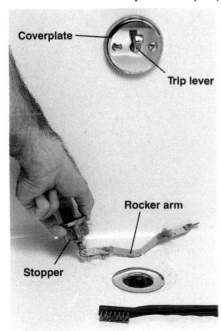

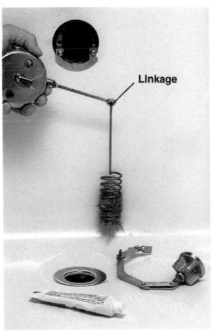

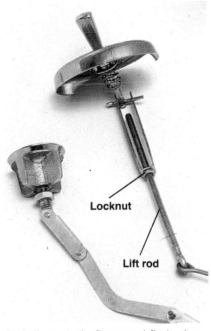

**1** Raise trip lever to the full open position. Carefully pull stopper and rocker arm assembly from drain opening. Clean hair or debris from rocker arm with a small wire brush.

**2** Remove screws from coverplate. Pull coverplate, trip lever, and linkage from overflow drain. Remove hair and debris. Remove corrosion with a small wire brush dipped in vinegar. Lubricate linkage with heatproof grease.

**3** Adjust drain flow and fix leaks by adjusting the linkage. Loosen locknut on threaded lift rod and screw lift rod up about 1/8". Tighten locknut and reinstall entire assembly.

# Clearing Clogged Drum Traps

In older homes, clogs in bathroom sinks or bathtubs may be caused by blockage in the drain lines connected to a drum trap. Remove the drum trap cover and use a hand auger to clear each drain line.

Drum traps usually are located in the floor next to the bathtub. They are identified by a flat, screw-in type cover or plug that is flush with the floor. Occasionally, a drum trap may be located under the floor. This type of drum trap will be positioned upside down so that the plug is accessible from below.

**A drum trap** is a canister made of lead or cast iron. Usually, more than one fixture drain line is connected to the drum. Drum traps are not vented, and they are no longer approved for new plumbing installations.

## Everything You Need:

Tools: adjustable wrench, hand auger.

Materials: rags or towels, penetrating oil, Teflon™ tape.

## How to Clear a Clogged Drum Trap

**1** Place rags or towels around the opening of the drum trap to absorb water that may be backed up in the lines.

**2** Remove the trap cover, using an adjustable wrench. Work carefully: older drum traps may be made of lead, which gets brittle with age. If cover does not unscrew easily, apply penetrating oil to lubricate the threads.

**3** Use a hand auger (pages 62 to 63) to clear each drain line. Then wrap the threads of the cover with Teflon™ tape and install. Flush all drains with hot water for five minutes.

# Clearing Clogged Floor Drains

When water backs up onto a basement floor, there is a clog in either the floor drain line, drain trap, or the sewer service line. Clogs in the drain line or trap may be cleared with a hand auger or a blow bag. To clear a sewer service line, see page 60.

Blow bags are especially useful for clearing clogs in floor drain lines. A blow bag attaches to a garden hose and is inserted directly into the floor drain line. The bag fills with water and then releases a powerful spurt that dislodges clogs.

**Everything You Need:**

Tools: adjustable wrench, screwdriver, hand auger, blow bag.

Materials: garden hose.

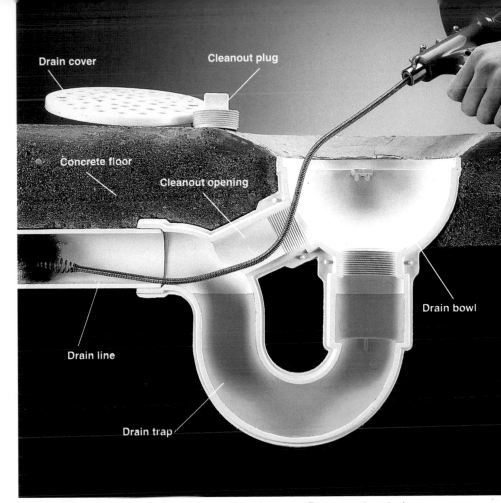

**Clear clogged floor drains** using a hand auger. Remove the drain cover, then use a wrench to unscrew the cleanout plug in the drain bowl. Push the auger cable through the cleanout opening directly into the drain line.

## How to Use a Blow Bag to Clear a Floor Drain

**1** Attach blow bag to garden hose, then attach hose to a hose bib or utility faucet.

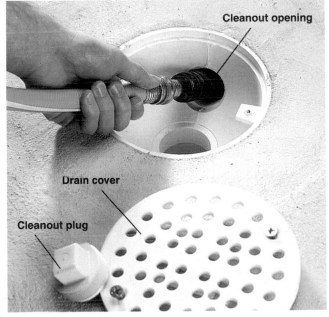

**2** Remove drain cover and cleanout plug. Insert the blow bag completely into the cleanout opening and turn on water. Allow several minutes for the blow bag to work properly.

# Clearing Clogs in Branch & Main Drain Lines

If using a plunger or a hand auger does not clear a clog in a fixture drain line, it means that the blockage may be in a branch drain line, the main waste and vent stack, or the sewer service line.

First, use an auger to clear the branch drain line closest to any stopped-up fixtures. Branch drain lines may be serviced through the cleanout fittings located at the end of the branch. Because waste water may be backed up in the drain lines, always open a cleanout with caution. Place a bucket and rags under the opening to catch waste water. Never position yourself directly under a cleanout opening while unscrewing the plug or cover.

If using an auger on the branch line does not solve the problem, then the clog may be located in a main waste and vent stack. To clear the stack, run an auger cable down through the roof vent. Make sure that the cable of your auger is long enough to reach down the entire length of the stack. If it is not, you may want to rent or borrow another auger. Always use extreme caution when working on a ladder or on a roof.

If no clog is present in the main stack, the problem may be located in the sewer service line. Locate the main cleanout, usually a Y-shaped fitting at the bottom of the main waste and vent stack. Remove the plug and push the cable of a hand auger into the opening.

Some sewer service lines in older homes have a house trap. The house trap is a U-shaped fitting located at the point where the sewer line exits the house. Most of the fitting will be beneath the floor surface, but it can be identified by its two openings. Use a hand auger to clean a house trap.

If the auger meets solid resistance in the sewer line, retrieve the cable and inspect the bit. Fine, hairlike roots on the bit indicate the line is clogged with tree roots. Dirt on the bit indicates a collapsed line.

Use a power auger to clear sewer service lines that are clogged with tree roots. Power augers are available at rental centers. However, a power auger is a large, heavy piece of equipment. Before renting, consider the cost of rental and the level of your do-it-yourself skills versus the price of a professional sewer cleaning service. If you rent a power auger, ask the rental dealer for complete instructions on how to operate the equipment.

Always consult a professional sewer cleaning service if you suspect a collapsed line.

**Everything You Need:**

Tools: adjustable wrench or pipe wrench, hand auger, cold chisel, ball peen hammer.

Materials: bucket, rags, penetrating oil, cleanout plug (if needed), pipe joint compound.

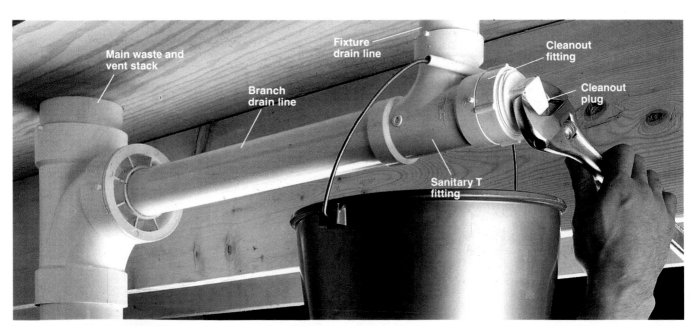

**Clear a branch drain line** by locating the cleanout fitting at the end of the line. Place a bucket underneath the opening to catch waste water, then slowly unscrew the cleanout plug with an adjustable wrench. Clear clogs in the branch drain line with a hand auger (pages 62 to 63).

**Clear the main waste and vent stack** by running the cable of a hand auger down through the roof vent. Always use extreme caution while working on a ladder or roof.

**Clear the house trap** in a sewer service line using a hand auger. Slowly remove only the plug on the "street side" of the trap. If water seeps out the opening as the plug is removed, the clog is in the sewer line beyond the trap. If no water seeps out, auger the trap. If no clog is present in the trap, replace the street-side plug and remove the house-side plug. Use the auger to clear clogs located between the house trap and main stack.

## How to Remove & Replace a Main Drain Cleanout Plug

**1** Remove the cleanout plug, using a large wrench. If plug does not turn out, apply penetrating oil around edge of plug, wait 10 minutes, and try again. Place rags and a bucket under fitting opening to catch any water that may be backed up in the line.

**2** Remove stubborn plugs by placing the cutting edge of chisel on edge of plug. Strike chisel with a ball peen hammer to move plug counterclockwise. If plug does not turn out, break it into pieces with the chisel and hammer. Remove all broken pieces.

**3** Replace old plug with new plastic plug. Apply pipe joint compound to the threads of the replacement plug and screw into cleanout fitting.

**Alternate:** Replace old plug with an expandable rubber plug. A wing nut squeezes the rubber core between two metal plates. The rubber bulges slightly to create a watertight seal.

## How to Clear a Fixture Drain Line with a Hand Auger

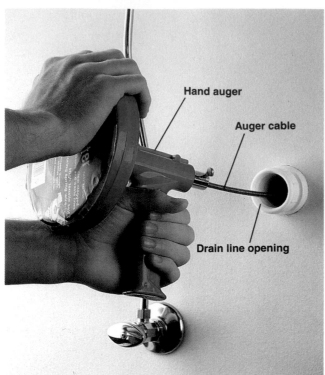

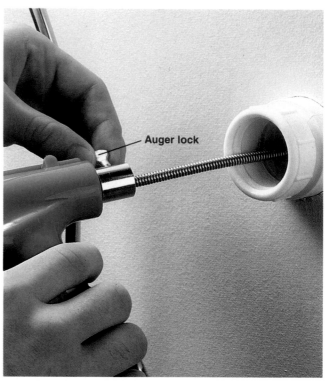

**1** Remove trap bend (page 52). Push the end of the auger cable into the drain line opening until resistance is met. This resistance usually indicates the end of the cable has reached a bend in the drain pipe.

**2** Set the auger lock so that at least 6" of cable extends out of the opening. Crank the auger handle in a clockwise direction to move the end of the cable past bend in drain line.

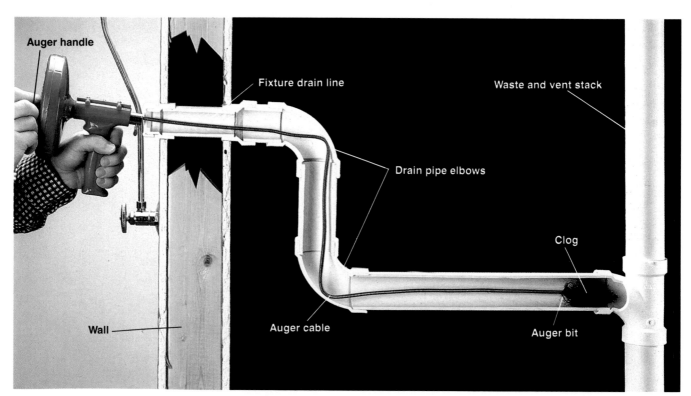

**3** Release the lock and continue pushing the cable into the opening until firm resistance is felt. Set the auger lock and crank the handle in a clockwise direction. Solid resistance that prevents the cable from advancing indicates a clog. Some clogs, such as a sponge or an accumulation of hair, can be snagged and retrieved (step 4). Continuous resistance that allows the cable to advance slowly is probably a soap clog (step 5).

**Hand grip**

**4** Pull an obstruction out of the line by releasing the auger lock and cranking the handle clockwise. If no object can be retrieved, reconnect the trap bend and use the auger to clear the nearest branch drain line or main waste and vent stack (pages 60 to 61).

**5** Continuous resistance indicates a soap clog. Bore through the clog by cranking the auger handle clockwise while applying steady pressure on the hand grip of the auger. Repeat the procedure two or three times, then retrieve the cable. Reconnect the trap bend and flush the system with hot tap water to remove debris.

Labels on diagram:

- Heat-saver nipple fitting
- Flue hat
- Flexible water connector
- (1) Hot water outlet
- Glass-lined tank
- (2) Dip tube
- Anode rod
- Pressure-relief valve
- Outer jacket
- (5) Flue
- Insulation
- (3) Thermostat
- Reset button
- (4) Gas burner
- Gas cock
- Control box
- Thermocouple
- Pilot gas tube
- Burner gas tube

**How a gas water heater works:** Hot water leaves tank through the **hot water outlet (1)** as fresh, cold water enters the water heater through the **dip tube (2).** As the water temperature drops, the **thermostat (3)** opens the gas valve, and the **gas burner (4)** is lighted by pilot flame. Exhaust gases are vented through **flue (5).** When water temperature reaches preset temperature, the thermostat closes gas valve, extinguishing burner. The thermocouple protects against gas leaks by automatically shutting off gas if pilot flame goes out. Anode rod protects tank lining from rust by attracting corrosive elements in the water. Pressure-relief valve guards against ruptures caused by steam buildup in tank.

# Fixing a Water Heater

Standard tank water heaters are designed so that repairs are simple. All water heats have convenient access panels that make it easy to replace worn-out parts. When buying new water heater parts, make sure the replacements match the specifications of your water heater. Most water heaters have a nameplate that lists the information needed, including the pressure rating of the tank, and the voltage and wattage ratings of the electric heating elements.

Many water heater problems can be avoided with routine yearly maintenance. Flush the water heater once a year, and test the pressure-relief valve. Set the thermostat at a lower water temperature to prevent heat damage to the tank. (Note: water temperature may affect the efficiency of automatic dishwashers. Check manufacturer's directions for recommended water temperature.) Water heaters last about 10 years on average, but with regular maintenance, a water heater can last 20 years or more.

Do not install an insulating jacket around a gas water heater. Insulation can block air supply and prevent the water heater from ventilating properly. Many water heater manufacturers prohibit the use of insulating jackets. To save energy, insulate the hot water pipes instead, using the materials described on page 70.

The pressure-relief valve is an important safety device that should be checked at least once each year and replaced, if needed. When replacing the pressure-relief valve, shut off the water and drain several gallons of water from the tank.

| Problems | Repairs |
|---|---|
| No hot water, or not enough hot water. | 1. **Gas heater:** Make sure gas is on, then relight pilot flame.<br>**Electric heater:** Make sure power is on, then reset thermostat.<br>2. Flush water heater to remove sediment in tank (photo, below).<br>3. Insulate hot water pipes to reduce heat loss (page 70).<br>4. **Gas heater:** Clean gas burner & replace thermocouple (pages 66 to 67).<br>**Electric heater:** Replace heating element or thermostat (pages 68 to 69).<br>5. Raise temperature setting of thermostat. |
| Pressure-relief valve leaks. | 1. Lower the temperature setting (photo, below).<br>2. Install a new pressure-relief valve. |
| Pilot flame will not stay lighted. | Clean gas burner & replace the thermocouple (pages 66 to 67). |
| Water heater leaks around base of tank. | Replace the water heater immediately. |

## Tips for Maintaining a Water Heater

**Flush the water heater** once a year by draining several gallons of water from the tank. Flushing removes sediment buildup that causes corrosion and reduces heating efficiency.

**Test pressure-relief valve** once a year. Lift up on lever and let it snap back. Valve should allow a burst of water into drain pipe. If not, install new valve.

**Lower the temperature** setting on thermostat to 120° F. Lower temperature setting reduces damage to tank caused by overheating, and also reduces energy use.

# Fixing a Gas Water Heater

If a gas water heater does not heat water, first remove the outer and inner access panels and make sure the pilot is lighted. During operation, the outer and inner access panels must be in place. Operating the water heater without the access panels may allow air drafts to blow out the pilot flame.

If the pilot will not light, it is probably because the thermocouple is worn out. The thermocouple is a safety device designed to shut off the gas automatically if the pilot flame goes out. The thermocouple is a thin copper wire that runs from the control box to the gas burner. New thermocouples are inexpensive, and can be installed in a few minutes.

If the gas burner does not light even though the pilot flame is working, or if the gas burns with a yellow, smoky flame, the burner and the pilot gas tube should be cleaned. Clean the burner and gas tube annually to improve energy efficiency and extend the life of the water heater.

A gas water heater must be well ventilated. If you smell smoke or fumes coming from a water heater, shut off the water heater and make sure the exhaust duct is not clogged with soot. A rusted duct must be replaced.

**Remember to shut off the gas before beginning work.**

### Everything You Need:

Tools: adjustable wrench, vacuum cleaner, needlenose pliers.

Materials: thin wire, replacement thermocouple.

## How to Clean a Gas Burner & Replace a Thermocouple

**1** Shut off gas by turning the gas cock on top of the control box to the OFF position. Wait 10 minutes for gas to dissipate.

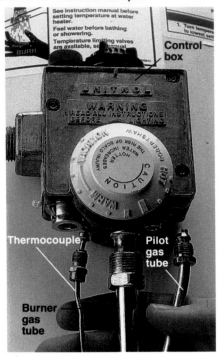

**2** Disconnect the pilot gas tube, the burner gas tube, and the thermocouple from the bottom of the control box, using an adjustable wrench.

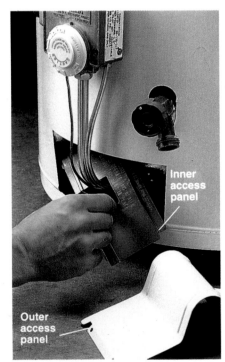

**3** Remove the outer and inner access panels covering the burner chamber.

**4** Pull down slightly on the pilot gas tube, the burner gas tube, and thermocouple wire to free them from the control box. Tilt the burner unit slightly and remove it from the burner chamber.

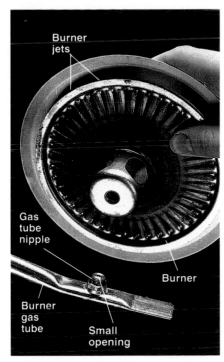

**5** Unscrew burner from burner gas tube nipple. Clean small opening in nipple, using a piece of thin wire. Vacuum out burner jets and the burner chamber.

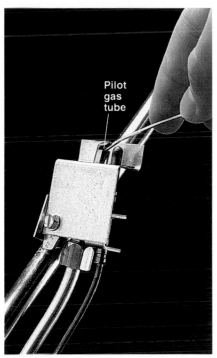

**6** Clean the pilot gas tube with a piece of wire. Vacuum out any loose particles. Screw burner onto gas tube nipple.

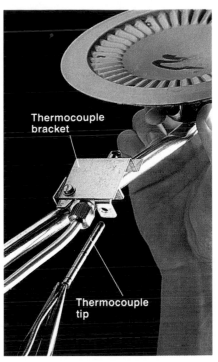

**7** Pull the old thermocouple from bracket. Install new thermocouple by pushing the tip into the bracket until it snaps into place.

**8** Insert the burner unit into the chamber. Flat tab at end of burner should fit into slotted opening in mounting bracket at the bottom of the chamber.

**9** Reconnect the gas tubes and the thermocouple to the control box. Turn on the gas and test for leaks. Light the pilot.

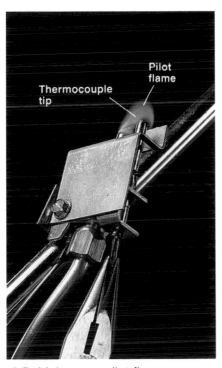

**10** Make sure pilot flame wraps around tip of thermocouple. If needed, adjust thermocouple with needlenose pliers until tip is in flame. Replace the inner and outer access panels.

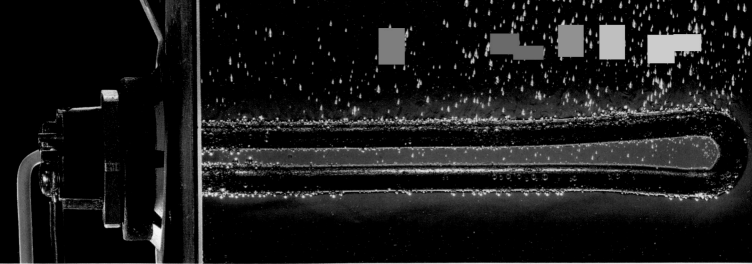

**Electric water heater** has one or two heating elements mounted in the side wall of the heater. Each element is connected to its own thermostat. When buying a replacement heating element or thermostat, make sure the replacement has same voltage and wattage rating as old part. This information is found on the nameplate.

# Fixing an Electric Water Heater

The most common problem with an electric water heater is a burned-out heating element. Many electric water heaters have two heating elements. To determine which element has failed, turn on a hot water faucet and test the temperature. If the water heater produces water that is warm, but not hot, replace the top heating element. If the heater produces a small amount of very hot water, followed by cold water, replace the bottom heating element.

If replacing the heating element does not solve the problem, then the thermostat may need to be replaced. These parts are found under convenient access panels on the side of the heater.

**Remember to turn off the power and test for current before touching wires.**

**Everything You Need:**

Tools: screwdriver, gloves, neon circuit tester, channel-type pliers.

Materials: masking tape, replacement heating element or thermostat, replacement gasket, pipe joint compound.

## How to Replace an Electric Thermostat

**1** Turn off power at main service panel. Remove access panel on side of heater, and **test for current.**

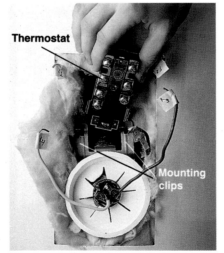

**2** Disconnect thermostat wires, and label connections with masking tape. Pull old thermostat out of mounting clips. Snap new thermostat into place, and reconnect wires.

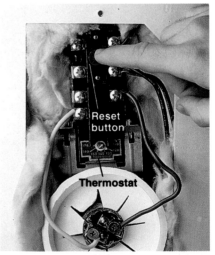

**3** Press thermostat reset button, then use a screwdriver to set thermostat to desired temperature. Replace insulation and access panel. Turn on power.

# How to Replace an Electric Heating Element

**1** Remove access panel on side of water heater. Shut off power to water heater. Close the shutoff valves, then drain the tank.

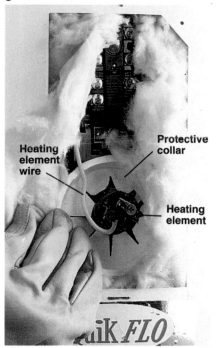

**2** Wearing protective gloves, carefully move insulation aside. **Caution: test for current,** then disconnect wires on heating element. Remove protective collar.

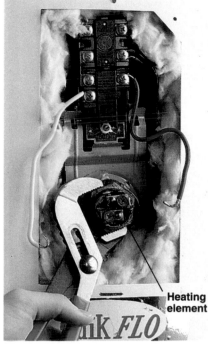

**3** Unscrew the heating element with channel-type pliers. Remove old gasket from around water heater opening. Coat both sides of new gasket with pipe joint compound.

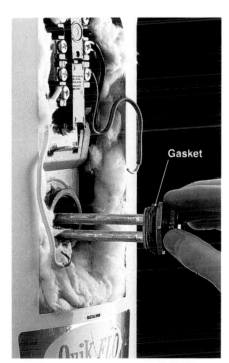

**4** Slide new gasket over heating element, and screw element into the tank. Tighten element with channel-type pliers.

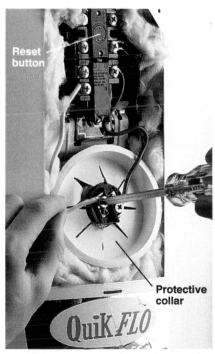

**5** Replace protective collar, and reconnect all wires. Turn on hot water faucets throughout house, then turn on water heater shutoff valves. When tap water runs steadily, close faucets.

**6** Use a screwdriver to set thermostat to desired temperature. Press thermostat reset buttons. Fold insulation over thermostat, and replace the access panel. Turn on power.

# Fixing Burst or Frozen Pipes

When a pipe bursts, immediately turn off the water at the main shutoff valve. Make temporary repairs with a sleeve clamp repair kit (page opposite).

A burst pipe is usually caused by freezing water. Prevent freezes by insulating pipes that run in crawl spaces or other unheated areas.

Pipes that freeze, but do not burst, will block water flow to faucets or appliances. Frozen pipes are easily thawed, but determining the exact location of the blockage may be difficult. Leave blocked faucets or valves turned on. Trace supply pipes that lead to blocked faucet or valve, and look for places where the line runs close to exterior walls or unheated areas. Thaw pipes with a heat gun or hair dryer (below).

Old fittings or corroded pipe also may leak or rupture. It is best to replace all of the old pipe, rather than repair small sections.

**Begin any emergency repair** by turning off water supply at main shutoff valve. The main shutoff valve is usually located near water meter.

### Everything You Need:

Tools: heat gun or hair dryer, gloves, metal file, screwdriver.

Materials: pipe insulation, sleeve clamp repair kit.

## How to Repair Pipes Blocked with Ice

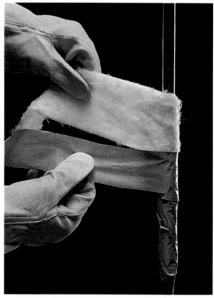

**1** Thaw pipes with a heat gun or hair dryer. Use heat gun on low setting, and keep nozzle moving to prevent overheating pipes.

**2** Let pipes cool, then insulate with sleeve-type foam insulation to prevent freezing. Use pipe insulation in crawl spaces or other unheated areas.

**Alternate:** Insulate pipes with fiberglass strip insulation and waterproof wrap. Wrap insulating strips loosely for best protection.

70

## How to Temporarily Fix a Burst Pipe

**1** Turn off water at main shutoff valve. Heat pipe gently with heat gun or hair dryer. Keep nozzle moving. Once frozen area is thawed, allow pipe to drain.

**2** Smooth rough edges of rupture with metal file.

**3** Place rubber sleeve of repair clamp around rupture. Make sure seam of sleeve is on opposite side of pipe from rupture.

**4** Place the two metal repair clamps around rubber sleeve.

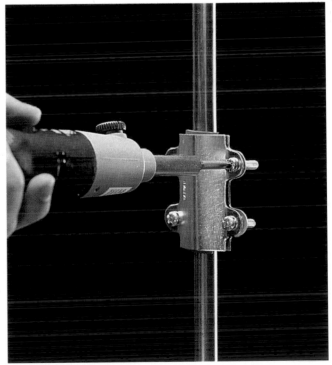

**5** Tighten screws with screwdriver. Open water supply and watch for leaks. If repair clamp leaks, retighten screws. **Caution: repairs made with a repair clamp kit are temporary.** Replace ruptured section of pipe as soon as possible.

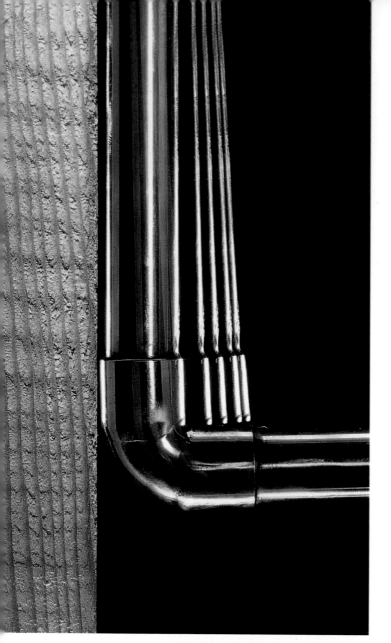

# Quieting Noisy Pipes

Pipes can make a loud banging noise when faucets are turned off or when valves on clothes washing machines (or other automatic appliances) shut abruptly. The sudden stop of flowing water creates a shock wave, called water hammer, that slams through the water supply system. Some pipes may knock against wall studs or joists, creating additional noise.

Stop water hammer by installing an air chamber. An air chamber is simply a vertical length of pipe installed in the supply line. An air chamber provides a cushion of air to absorb the shock wave of water hammer. More than one air chamber may be needed to stop water hammer completely.

In time, air in an air chamber may be displaced by water in the pipes. To restore the air in the chamber, drain the water supply system. When the system is refilled, the air will be restored.

Pipes that bang against studs or joists can be quieted by cushioning them with pieces of pipe insulation. Make sure pipe hangers are snug and that pipes are well supported.

**Everything You Need:**

Tools: utility knife, reciprocating saw or hacksaw, propane torch (for sweating copper), pipe wrenches (for galvanized iron).

Materials: foam rubber pipe insulation, pipe and fittings as needed.

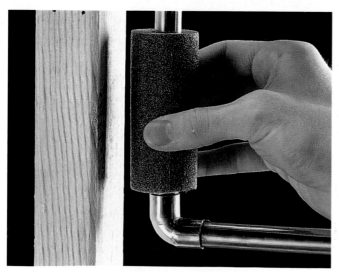

**Install cushions** made from pieces of foam rubber pipe insulation to prevent pipes from banging against wall studs or joists.

**Loose pipes** may bang or rub against joist hangers, creating unwanted noises. Use pieces of foam rubber pipe insulation to cushion pipes.

# How to Install an Air Chamber

**1** Shut off water supply and drain pipes. Measure and cut out a section of horizontal pipe for T-fitting.

**2** Install T-fitting in upright position.

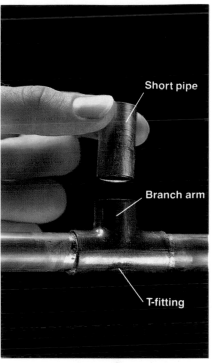

**3** Install a short piece of pipe in the branch arm of the T-fitting. This short pipe will be necessary to attach reducer fitting (step 4).

Short pipe

Branch arm

T-fitting

**4** Install reducer fitting. Use reducer to make sure diameter of air chamber pipe is larger than supply pipe.

Reducer fitting

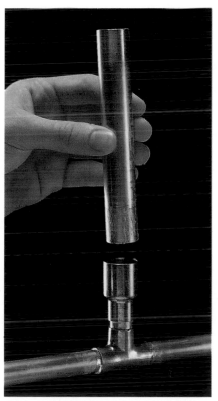

**5** Install 12" long section of pipe for air chamber.

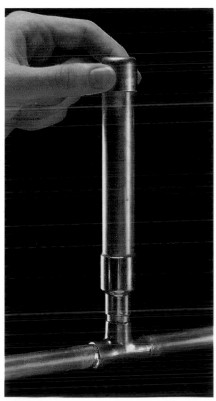

**6** Add cap to air chamber. Turn on water supply.

# Electrical Repairs

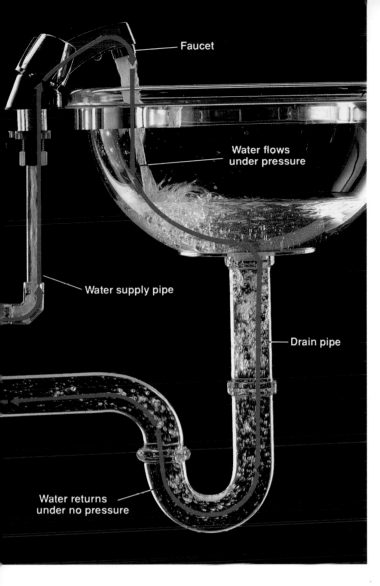

Faucet

Water flows
under pressure

Water supply pipe

Drain pipe

Water returns
under no pressure

# Understanding Electricity

A household electrical system can be compared with a home's plumbing system. Electrical current flows in wires in much the same way that water flows inside pipes. Both electricity and water enter the home, are distributed throughout the house, do their "work," and then exit.

In plumbing, water first flows through the pressurized water supply system. In electricity, current first flows along hot wires. Current flowing along hot wires also is pressurized. The pressure of electrical current is called **voltage**.

Large supply pipes can carry a greater volume of water than small pipes. Likewise, large electrical wires carry more current than small wires. This current-carrying capacity of wires is called **amperage**.

Water is made available for use through the faucets, spigots, and shower heads in a home. Electricity is made available through receptacles, switches, and fixtures.

Water finally leaves the home through a drain system, which is not pressurized. Similarly, electrical current flows back through neutral wires. The current in neutral wires is not pressurized, and is said to be at zero voltage.

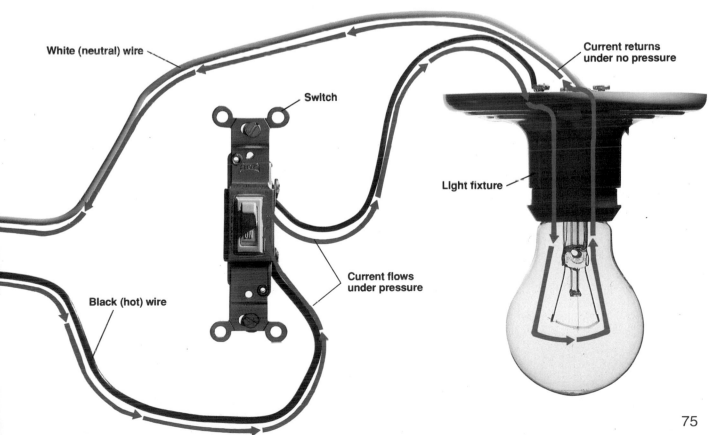

White (neutral) wire

Current returns
under no pressure

Switch

Light fixture

Current flows
under pressure

Black (hot) wire

# Your Electrical System

Electrical power that enters the home is produced by large **power plants**. Power plants are located in all parts of the country, and generate electricity with turbines that are turned by water, wind, or steam. From these plants electricity enters large "step-up" transformers that increase voltage to half a million volts or more.

Electricity flows easily at these large voltages, and travels through high-voltage transmission lines to communities that can be hundreds of miles from the power plants. "Step-down" transformers located at **substations** then reduce the voltage for distribution along street lines. On **utility power poles**, smaller transformers further reduce the voltage to ordinary 120-volt current for household use.

Lines carrying current to the house either run underground, or are strung overhead and attached to a post called a **service head**. Most homes built after 1950 have three wires running to the service head: two power lines, each carrying 120 volts of current, and a grounded neutral wire. Power from the two 120-volt lines may be combined at the **service panel** to supply current to large, 240-volt appliances like clothes dryers or electric water heaters.

Many older homes have only two wires running to the service head, with one 120-volt line and a grounded neutral wire. This older two-wire service is inadequate for the greater electricity requirements of today's homes. Contact an electrical contractor and your local power utility company to upgrade to a three-wire service.

Incoming power passes through an electric meter that measures power consumption. Power then enters the service panel, where it is distributed to circuits that run throughout the house. The service panel also contains fuses or circuit breakers that shut off power to the individual circuits in the event of a short circuit or an overload. Certain high-wattage appliances, like microwave ovens, are usually plugged into their own individual (dedicated) circuits to prevent overloads.

Voltage ratings determined by power companies and manufacturers have changed over the years. Current rated at 110 volts changed to 115 volts, then 120 volts. Current rated at 220 volts changed to 230 volts, then 240 volts. Similarly, ratings for receptacles, tools, light fixtures, and appliances have changed from 115 volts to 125 volts. These changes will not affect the performance of new devices connected to older wiring. For making electrical calculations, use a rating of 120 volts or 240 volts for your circuits.

**Power plants** supply electricity to thousands of homes and businesses. Step-up transformers increase the voltage produced at the plant, making the power flow more easily along high-voltage transmission lines.

**Substations** are located near the communities they serve. A typical substation takes current from high-voltage transmission lines and reduces it for distribution along street lines.

**Utility pole transformers** reduce the high-voltage current that flows through power lines along neighborhood streets. A utility pole transformer reduces voltage from 10,000 volts to the normal 120-volt current used in households.

**Service head** or weather head anchors the service wires and prevents moisture from entering the house.

**Service wires** supply electricity to the house from the utility company's power lines.

**Chandelier**

**Switch loop**

**Wall switch**

**Separate 120-volt circuit** for microwave oven.

**Receptacles**

**GFCI receptacles**

**Electric meter** measures the amount of electrical power consumed, and displays the measurement inside a glass dome.

**Separate 240-volt circuit** for water heater.

**Service panel** distributes electrical power into circuits.

**Grounding rod** must be at least 8 feet long and is driven into the ground outside the house.

**Grounding wire** to metal grounding rod.

**Separate 120/240-volt** circuit for clothes dryer.

**Grounding wire** to metal water pipe.

**Jumper wire** is used to bypass the water meter and ensures an uninterrupted grounding pathway.

## Parts of the Electrical System

**The service head**, sometimes called the weather head, anchors the service wires to the home. Three wires provide the standard 240-volt service necessary for the average home. Older homes may have two-wire service that provides only 120 volts of power. Two-wire service should be upgraded to three-wire service by an electrical contractor.

**The electric meter** measures the amount of electrical power consumed. It is usually attached to the side of the house, and connects to the service head. A thin metal disc inside the meter rotates when power is used. The electric meter belongs to your local power utility company. If you suspect the meter is not functioning properly, contact the power company.

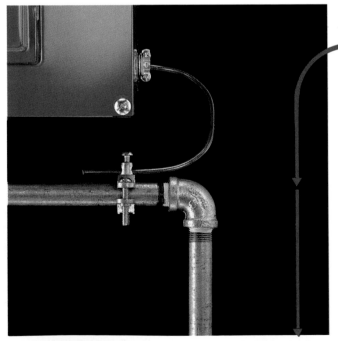

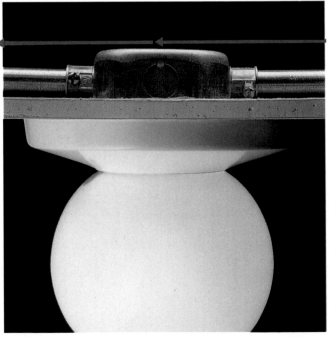

**Grounding wire** connects the electrical system to the earth through a cold water pipe and a grounding rod. In the event of an overload or short circuit, the grounding wire allows excess electrical power to find its way harmlessly to the earth.

**Light fixtures** attach directly to a household electrical system. They are usually controlled with wall switches. The two common types of light fixtures are incandescent (page 124) and fluorescent (page 134).

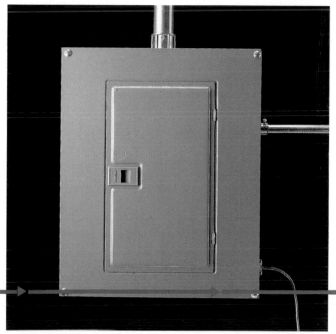

**The main service panel,** sometimes called a fuse box or **breaker box,** distributes power to individual circuits. Fuses or circuit breakers protect each circuit from short circuits and overloads. Fuses and circuit breakers also are used to shut off power to individual circuits while repairs are made.

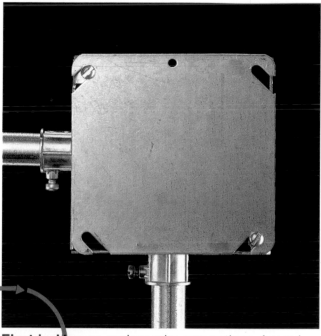

**Electrical boxes** enclose wire connections. According to the National Electrical Code, all wire splices or connections must be contained entirely in a plastic or metal electrical box.

**Switches** control electrical current passing through hot circuit wires. Switches can be wired to control light fixtures, ceiling fans, appliances, and receptacles.

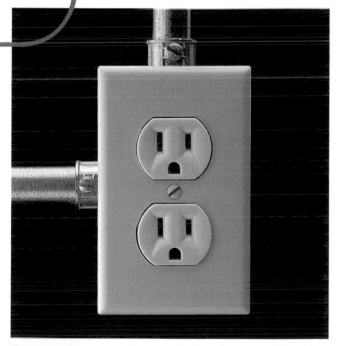

**Receptacles,** sometimes called **outlets,** provide plug-in access to electrical power. A 125-volt, 15-amp receptacle with a grounding hole is the most typical receptacle in wiring systems installed after 1965. Most receptacles have two plug-in locations, and are called **duplex receptacles.**

# Understanding Circuits

An electrical circuit is a continuous loop. Household circuits carry power from the main service panel, throughout the house, and back to the main service panel. Several switches, receptacles, light fixtures, or appliances may be connected to a single circuit.

Current enters a circuit loop on hot wires, and returns along neutral wires. These wires are color coded for easy identification. Hot wires are black or red, and neutral wires are white or light gray. For safety, most circuits include a bare copper or green insulated grounding wire. The grounding wire conducts current in the event of a short circuit or overload, and helps reduce the chance of severe electrical shock. The service panel also has a grounding wire connected to a metal water pipe and metal grounding rod buried underground (pages 82 to 83).

If a circuit carries too much power, it can overload. A fuse or a circuit breaker protects each circuit in case of overloads (pages 94 to 95).

Current returns to the service panel along a neutral circuit wire. Current then becomes part of a main circuit and leaves the house on a large neutral service wire that returns it to the utility pole transformer.

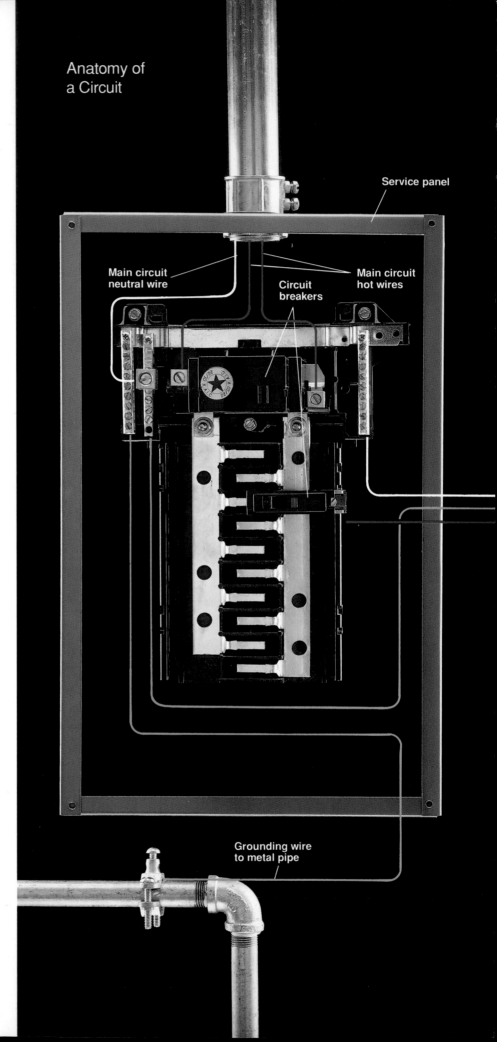

Anatomy of a Circuit

Service panel

Main circuit neutral wire

Circuit breakers

Main circuit hot wires

Grounding wire to metal pipe

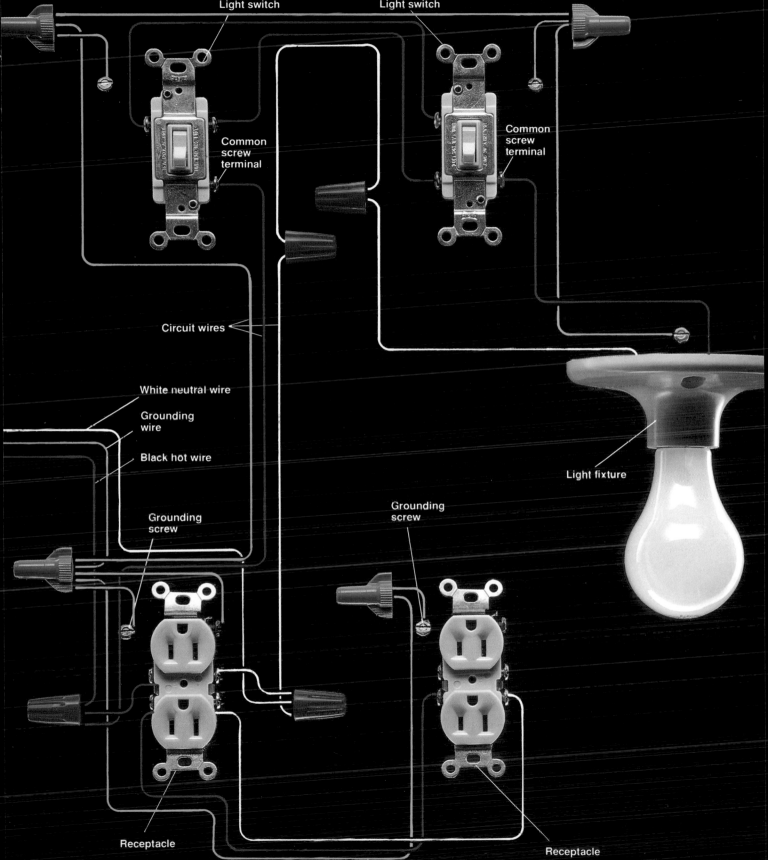

Light switch

Light switch

Common
screw
terminal

Common
screw
terminal

Circuit wires

White neutral wire

Grounding
wire

Black hot wire

Grounding
screw

Grounding
screw

Light fixture

Receptacle

Receptacle

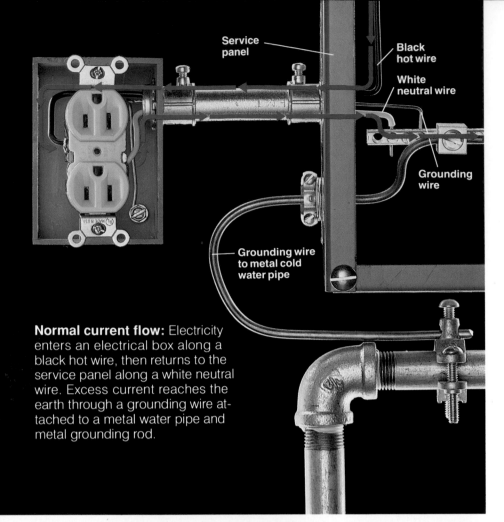

Service panel

Black hot wire

White neutral wire

Grounding wire

Grounding wire to metal cold water pipe

**Normal current flow:** Electricity enters an electrical box along a black hot wire, then returns to the service panel along a white neutral wire. Excess current reaches the earth through a grounding wire attached to a metal water pipe and metal grounding rod.

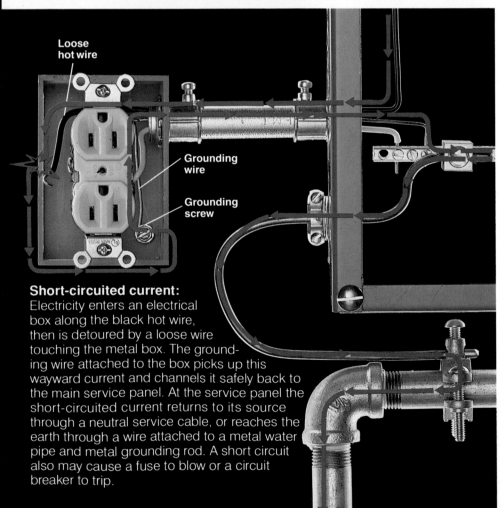

Loose hot wire

Grounding wire

Grounding screw

**Short-circuited current:** Electricity enters an electrical box along the black hot wire, then is detoured by a loose wire touching the metal box. The grounding wire attached to the box picks up this wayward current and channels it safely back to the main service panel. At the service panel the short-circuited current returns to its source through a neutral service cable, or reaches the earth through a wire attached to a metal water pipe and metal grounding rod. A short circuit also may cause a fuse to blow or a circuit breaker to trip.

# Grounding & Polarization

Electricity always seeks to return to its source and complete a continuous circuit. In a household wiring system, this return path is provided by white neutral wires that return current to the main service panel. From the service panel, current returns along a neutral service wire to a power pole transformer.

A **grounding wire** provides an additional return path for electrical current. The grounding wire is a safety feature. It is designed to conduct electricity if current seeks to return to the service panel along a path other than the neutral wire, a condition known as a **short circuit**.

A short circuit is a potentially dangerous situation. If an electrical box, tool or appliance becomes short circuited and is touched by a person, the electrical current may attempt to return to its source by passing through that person's body.

However, electrical current always seeks to move along the easiest path. A grounding wire provides a safe, easy path for current to follow back to its source. If a person touches an electrical box, tool, or appliance that has a properly installed grounding wire, any chance of receiving a severe electrical shock is greatly reduced.

In addition, household wiring systems are required to be connected directly to the earth. The earth has a unique ability to absorb the electrons of electrical current. In the event of a short circuit or overload, any excess electricity will find its way along the grounding wire to the earth, where it becomes harmless.

This additional grounding is completed by wiring the household electrical system to a metal cold water pipe and a metal grounding rod that is buried underground.

After 1920, most American homes included receptacles that accepted **polarized plugs.** While not a true grounding method, the two-slot polarized plug and receptacle was designed to keep hot current flowing along black or red wires, and neutral current flowing along white or gray wires.

Armored cable and metal conduit, widely installed in homes during the 1940s, provided a true grounding path. When connected to metal junction boxes, it provided a metal pathway back to the service panel.

Modern cable includes a bare or green insulated copper wire that serves as the grounding path. This grounding wire is connected to all receptacles and metal boxes to provide a continuous pathway for any short-circuited current. A cable with a grounding wire usually is attached to three-slot receptacles. By plugging a three-prong plug into a grounded three-slot receptacle, appliances and tools are protected from short circuits.

Use a receptacle adapter to plug three-prong plugs into two-slot receptacles, but use it only if the receptacle connects to a grounding wire or grounded electrical box. Adapters have short grounding wires or wire loops that attach to the receptacle's coverplate mounting screw. The mounting screw connects the adapter to the grounded metal electrical box.

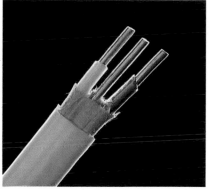

**Modern NM (nonmetallic) cable,** found in most wiring systems installed after 1965, contains a bare copper wire that provides grounding for receptacle and switch boxes.

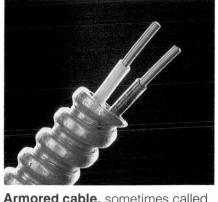

**Armored cable,** sometimes called BX or Greenfield cable, has a metal sheath that serves as the grounding pathway. Short-circuited current flows through the metal sheath back to the service panel.

**Polarized receptacles** have a long slot and a short slot. Used with a polarized plug, the polarized receptacle keeps electrical current directed for safety.

**Three-slot receptacles** are required by code for new homes. They are usually connected to a standard two-wire cable with ground (above, left).

**Receptacle adapter** allows three-prong plugs to be inserted into two-slot receptacles. The adapter can be used only with grounded receptacles, and the grounding loop or wire of the adapter must be attached to the coverplate mounting screw of the receptacle.

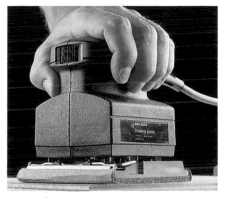

**Double-insulated tools** have nonconductive plastic bodies to prevent shocks caused by short circuits. Because of these features, double-insulated tools can be used safely with ungrounded receptacles.

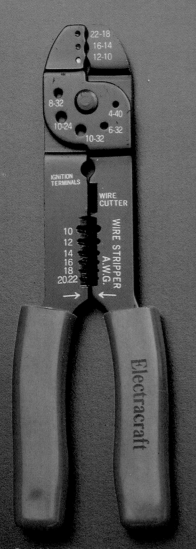

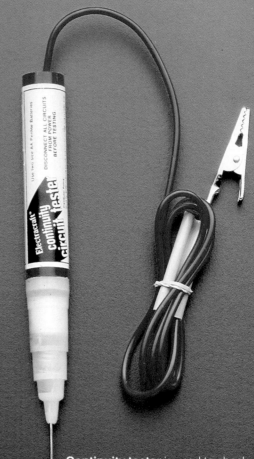

**Needlenose pliers** bends and shapes wires for making screw terminal connections. Some needlenose pliers also have cutting jaws for clipping wires.

**Combination tool** is essential for home wiring projects. It cuts cables and individual wires, measures wire gauges, and strips the insulation from wires. It has insulated handles.

**Continuity tester** is used to check switches, lighting fixtures, and other devices for faults. It has a battery that generates current, and a loop of wire for creating an electrical circuit (page 110).

**Cordless screwdriver** drives a wide variety of screws and fasteners. It is rechargeable, and can be used in either a power or manual mode. A removable tip allows the cordless screwdriver to drive either slotted or Phillips screws.

**Neon circuit tester** is used to check circuit wires for power. Testing for power is an essential safety step in any electrical repair project (page 120).

# Tools for Electrical Repairs

Home electrical repairs require only a few inexpensive tools. As with any tool purchase, invest in quality when buying tools for electrical repairs.

Keep tools clean and dry, and store them securely. Tools with cutting jaws, like needlenose pliers and combination tools, should be resharpened or discarded if the cutting edges become dull.

Several testing tools are used in electrical repair projects. Neon circuit testers (page 120), continuity testers (page 110), and multi-testers (below) should be checked periodically to make sure they are operating properly. Continuity testers and multi-testers have batteries that should be replaced regularly.

**Insulated screwdrivers** have rubber-coated handles that reduce the risk of shock if the screwdriver should accidentally touch live wires.

**Fuse puller** is used to remove cartridge-type fuses from the fuse blocks usually found in older main service panels.

**Cable ripper** fits over NM (nonmetallic) cable. A small cutting point rips the outer plastic vinyl sheath on NM cable so the sheath can be removed without damaging wires.

**Multi-tester** is a versatile, battery-operated tool frequently used to measure electrical voltages. It also is used to test for continuity in switches, light fixtures, and other electrical devices. An adjustable control makes it possible to measure current ranging from 1 to 1000 volts. A multi-tester is an essential tool for measuring current in low-voltage transformers, like those used to power doorbell and thermostat systems (pages 144 to 157).

# Electricity & Safety

Safety should be the primary concern of anyone working with electricity. Although most household electrical repairs are simple and straightforward, always use caution and good judgment when working with electrical wiring or devices. Common sense can prevent accidents.

The basic rule of electrical safety is **always turn off power to the area or device you are working on.** At the main service panel, remove the fuse or shut off the circuit breaker that controls the circuit you are servicing. Then check to make sure the power is off by testing for power with a neon circuit tester (page 84). Restore power only when the repair or replacement project is complete.

Electricity is dangerous only if it flows outside the established wiring system. By nature, electricity seeks to return to earth along the easiest path. If power "leaks" and finds a path outside the circuit wires (through you or structural members in your house) shock or fire can occur.

## How to Shut Off Electricity Before Making Repairs

**Circuit breakers** control current load in newer systems. Identify breaker controlling wires you will touch. Switch breaker to OFF. **Test wires with circuit tester** before beginning repair.

**Fuses** control current load in older wiring systems. Identify the fuse controlling wires you will touch. **Touching insulated rim only,** unscrew fuse and set aside. **Test wires with circuit tester** before beginning repair.

**Cartridge fuses** protect circuits for larger appliances. **Use one hand only** to open panel and handle fuses. If fuse is housed in a block, grip handle of block and pull. Remove fuse from clips using fuse puller.

To prevent this type of power leak—known as a short circuit—your electrical network depends on a ground system (pages 82 to 83). If circuit wires fail, the ground system provides a controlled route for electricity to follow. In newer wiring, bare copper or insulated green wires run through the system. These are ground wires. They are connected, through the service panel, to the earth. When making electrical repairs, always reconnect the ground wires. Before replacing an older 2-prong outlet receptacle with a new 3-prong model, always check the system to see if it is grounded (page 89). A 3- prong outlet receptacle will not provide grounding protection unless it is connected to a grounded system.

If a fuse blows or a circuit breaker trips, there is either a short circuit or an overloaded circuit. An overloaded circuit means that lights and appliances are drawing more power than the circuit can safely handle. Move appliances to other circuits, then either replace the fuse or switch the lever of the tripped breaker fully to OFF, then to ON. Try to arrange the appliances on circuits so that power usage is balanced to keep from overloading any one circuit. If a fuse blows or breaker trips immediately after being replaced or reset, there may be a short circuit. With the power off, you can open up all the switch, receptacle or fixture boxes on the circuit to see if there is a wire that has come loose; or you can test the switches (page 110), receptacles (page 120) and fixtures (page 124) to see if they need replacement. If you cannot find the short circuit, call an electrician immediately.

Follow the safety tips shown on these pages. Never attempt an electrical project beyond your skill or confidence level. Never attempt to repair or replace your main service panel or service entrance head (pages 78 to 79). These are jobs for a qualified electrician and require that the power company shuts off power to your house.

**Shut off power** to the proper circuit at the fuse box or main service panel before beginning work.

**Make a map** of your household electrical circuits to help you turn the proper circuits on and off for electrical repairs.

**Close service panel door** and post a warning sign to prevent others from turning on power while you are working on electrical projects.

**Wear rubber-soled shoes** while working on electrical projects. On damp floors, stand on a rubber mat or dry wooden boards.

**Use fiberglass or wood ladders** when making routine household repairs near the service head.

**Keep a flashlight** near your main service panel. Check flashlight batteries regularly.

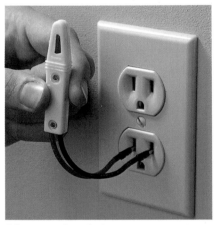

**Always check for power** at the fixture you are servicing before you begin any work.

**Use extension cords** only for temporary connections. Never place them underneath rugs, or fasten them to walls, baseboards, or other surfaces.

**Use correct fuses or breakers** in the main service panel (pages 94 to 95). Never install a fuse or breaker that has a higher amperage rating than the circuit wires.

**Do not touch metal pipes,** faucets, or fixtures while working with electricity. The metal may provide a grounding path, allowing electrical current to flow through your body.

**Never alter the prongs** of a plug to fit a receptacle. If possible, install a new grounded receptacle.

**Do not drill walls or ceilings** without first shutting off electrical power to the circuits that may be hidden. Use double-insulated tools.

## Electrical Safety Tips

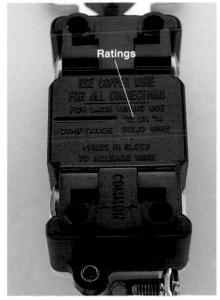

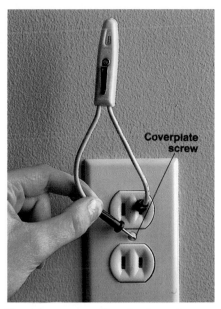

**Read markings** on old outlet and switches before buying replacements. Choose replacements with the same voltage and amp ratings. If you have aluminum wiring, or if the old outlet or switch is marked CO/ALR, select a similar replacement.

**Test for grounding** by inserting one probe of neon circuit tester in a vertical slot. Touch other probe to metal coverplate screw. Repeat test with other vertical slot. If tester lights, outlet is grounded, and a new 3-slot receptacle can be installed (page 122).

**Install GFCI** (ground-fault circuit interrupter) whenever replacing a receptacle near water or plumbing, or outside. A GFCI detects changes in current flow and quickly shuts off electricity in outlet before shock can occur. Install GFCI receptacles in laundry rooms, bathrooms, kitchen or outdoor outlets.

**Three-prong plugs** should be used only in a properly grounded outlet. If using a 3-prong adapter, test to make sure it is grounded. Do not alter the plug to fit a 2-slot receptacle.

**Polarized plugs** use prongs of different width to maintain proper circuit continuity and protect against shock. If you have a receptacle that will not accept polarized plugs, do not alter the plugs to fit the outlet. Install a new receptacle (page 122) after testing outlet for grounding.

**Protect children** against the possibility of electrical shock. Place tight protective caps in any receptacles that are not being used.

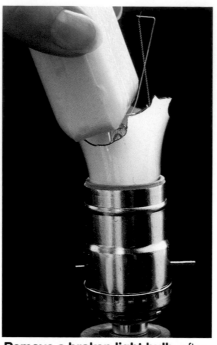

**Dry your hands** before plugging in or unplugging appliances. Water conducts electricity and increases the possibility of shock.

**Remove a broken light bulb,** after turning off electricity or unplugging lamp, by inserting a bar of soap, then turning counterclockwise. Discard soap. Or use needlenose pliers to grip filament or metal base of bulb.

**Mark the wires** with small tabs of masking tape before disconnecting an old receptacle or switch. Attach wires to new receptacle or switch using tape marks as a guide.

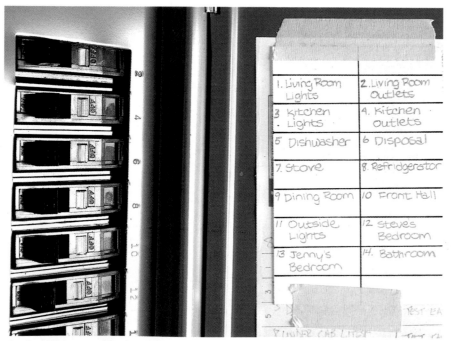

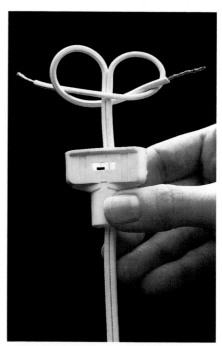

**A circuit map** can simplify repairs. Shut off power to one circuit at a time (page 86). For each circuit, check throughout the house and make a list of which outlets, appliances and lights do not carry power. Tape a description of the circuits on the door of the service panel. Write the circuit number on the back of outlet and switch coverplates.

**Tie an underwriter's knot** as shown when replacing an electrical plug or cord, if there is space in the plug body. This prevents the wires from being pulled from the plug.

# Glossary of Electrical Terms

**Ampacity:** A measurement of how many amps can be safely carried by a wire or cable to a light, tool, or an appliance. Ampacity varies according to the diameter of the wire (page 97).

**Armored cable:** Two or more wires that are grouped together and protected by a flexible metal covering.

**Box:** A device used to contain wiring connections.

**BX:** See **armored cable.**

**Cable:** Two or more wires that are grouped together and protected by a covering or sheath.

**Circuit:** A continuous loop of electrical current flowing along wires or cables that begins and ends at the service panel.

**Circuit breaker:** A safety device that interrupts an electrical circuit in the event of an overload or short circuit.

**Common wire:** The hot circuit wire that brings current from the power source to a three-way switch, or that carries current from a three-way switch to a light fixture. A common wire is always connected to the darker screw terminal on the switch, sometimes labeled COMMON.

**Conductor:** Any material that allows electrical current to flow through it. Copper wire is an especially good conductor.

**Conduit:** A metal or plastic tube used to protect wires.

**Continuity:** An uninterrupted electrical pathway through a circuit or electrical fixture.

**Current:** The movement of electrons along a conductor.

**Dedicated circuit:** An electrical circuit that serves only one appliance or series of electric heaters.

**Duplex receptacle:** A receptacle that provides connections for two plugs.

**EMT:** *Electrical Metallic Tubing.* A type of metal conduit used for exposed indoor wiring installations, such as wiring in an unfinished basement.

**Feeder cable:** The length of cable that carries power from the main circuit breaker panel to the first electrical box in a circuit, or from the main panel to a circuit breaker subpanel. Also known as a *home run.*

**Fuse:** A safety device, usually found in older homes, that interrupts electrical circuits during an overload or short circuit.

**GFCI:** A duplex receptacle or circuit breaker rated as a *Ground-Fault Circuit-Interrupter.* GFCI receptacles provide extra protection against shock and are required by Code in some locations.

**Greenfield:** See **armored cable.**

**Grounded wire:** See **neutral wire.**

**Grounding wire:** A wire used in an electrical circuit to conduct current to the earth in the event of a short circuit. The grounding wire often is a bare copper wire.

**Hot wire:** Any wire that carries voltage. In an electrical circuit, the hot wire usually is covered with black or red insulation.

**Insulator:** Any material, such as plastic or rubber, that resists the flow of electrical current. Insulating materials protect wires and cables.

**Junction box:** See **box.**

**Line side wires:** Circuit wires that extend "upstream" from an electrical box, toward the power source.

**Load side wires:** Circuit wires extending "downstream" from an electrical box toward end of circuit.

**Meter:** A device used to measure the amount of electrical power being used.

**Neutral wire:** A wire that returns current at zero voltage to the source of electrical power. Usually covered with white or light gray insulation. Also called the grounded wire.

**NM cable:** *Non-Metallic sheathed cable.* The standard cable used for indoor wiring inside finished walls.

**Outlet:** See **receptacle.**

**Overload:** A demand for more current than the circuit wires or electrical device was designed to carry. Usually causes a fuse to blow or a circuit breaker to trip.

**Pigtail:** A short length of wire used to join two or more circuit wires to the same screw terminal on a receptacle, switch, or metal electrical box. Pigtails are color-coded to match the wires they are connected to.

**Polarized receptacle:** A receptacle designed to keep hot current flowing along black or red wires, and neutral current flowing along white or gray wires.

**Power:** The result of hot current flowing for a period of time. Use of power makes heat, motion, or light.

**Receptacle:** A device that provides plug-in access to electrical power.

**Romex:** A brand name of plastic-sheathed electrical cable (see **NM cable**) that is commonly used for indoor wiring.

**Screw terminal:** A place where a wire connects to a receptacle, switch, or fixture.

**Service panel:** A metal box usually near the site where electrical power enters the house. In the service panel, electrical current is split into individual circuits. The service panel has circuit breakers or fuses to protect each circuit.

**Short circuit:** An accidental and improper contact between tow current-carrying wires, or between a current-carrying wire and a grounding conductor. A short circuit will blow a fuse or trip a circuit breaker.

**Split receptacle:** A duplex receptacle in which the connecting tab linking the brass screw terminals has been broken. A split receptacle is required when one half of a duplex receptacle is controlled by a switch, or when each half is controlled by a different circuit.

**Switch:** A device that controls electrical current passing through hot circuit wires. Used to turn lights and appliances on and off.

**Three-wire cable:** Sheathed cable with one black, one white, and one red insulated conductor, plus a bare copper grounding wire.

**Traveler wires:** In a three-way switch configuration, two *traveler wires* run between the pairs of traveler screw terminals on the three-way switches.

**Two-wire cable:** Sheathed cable with one black and one white insulated conductor plus a bare copper grounding wire.

**UF cable:** *Underground Feeder* cable. Used for outdoor wiring, UF cable is rated for direct contact with soil.

**UL:** An abbreviation for Underwriters Laboratories, an organization that tests electrical devices and manufactured products for safety.

**Voltage** (or **volts**): A measurement of electricity in terms of pressure.

**Wattage** (or **watt**): A measurement of electrical power in terms of total energy consumed. Watts can be calculated by multiplying the voltage times the amps.

**Wire nut:** A device used to connect two or more wires together.

# Service Panels

Every home has a main service panel that distributes electrical current to the individual circuits. The main service panel usually is found in the basement, garage, or utility area, and can be identified by its metal casing. Before making any repair to your electrical system, you must shut off power to the correct circuit at the main service panel. The service panel should be indexed (page 90) so circuits can be identified easily.

Service panels vary in appearance, depending on the age of the system. Very old wiring may operate on 30-amp service that has only two circuits. New homes can have 200-amp service with 30 or more circuits. Find the size of the service by reading the amperage rating printed on the main fuse block or main circuit breaker.

Regardless of age, all service panels have **fuses** or **circuit breakers** (pages 94 to 95) that control each circuit and protect them from overloads. In general, older service panels use fuses, while newer service panels use circuit breakers.

In addition to the main service panel, your electrical system may have a subpanel that controls some of the circuits in the home. A subpanel has its own circuit breakers or fuses, and is installed to control circuits that have been added to an existing wiring system.

The subpanel resembles the main service panel, but is usually smaller. It may be located near the main panel, or it may be found near the areas served by the new circuits. Garages and attics that have been updated often have their own subpanels. If your home has a subpanel, make sure that its circuits are indexed correctly.

When handling fuses or circuit breakers, make sure the area around the service panel is dry. Never remove the protective cover on the service panel. After turning off a circuit to make electrical repairs, remember to always test the circuit for power before touching any wires.

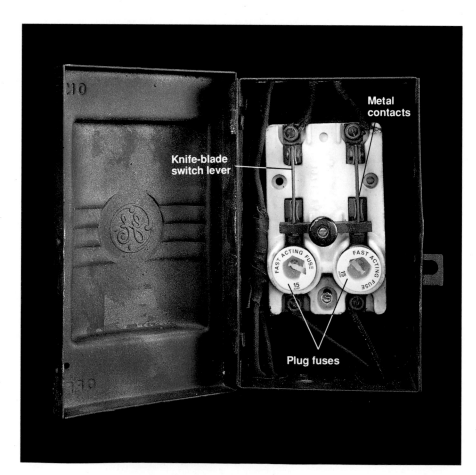

Knife-blade switch lever

Metal contacts

Plug fuses

**A 30-amp service panel**, common in systems installed before 1950, is identified by a ceramic fuse holder containing two plug fuses and a "knife-blade" switch lever. The fuse holder sometimes is contained in a black metal box mounted in an entryway or basement. This 30-amp service panel provides only 120 volts of power, and now is considered inadequate. For example, most home loan programs, like the FHA (Federal Housing Administration), require that 30-amp service be updated to 100 amps or more before a home can qualify for mortgage financing.

To shut off power to individual circuits in a 30-amp panel, carefully unscrew the plug fuses, touching only the insulated rim of the fuse. To shut off power to the entire house, open the knife-blade switch. Be careful not to touch the metal contacts on the switch.

**A 60-amp fuse panel** often is found in wiring systems installed between 1950 and 1965. It usually is housed in a gray metal cabinet that contains four individual plug fuses, plus one or two pull-out fuse blocks that hold cartridge fuses. This type of panel is regarded as adequate for a small, 1100-square-foot house that has no more than one 240-volt appliance. Many homeowners update 60-amp service to 100 amps or more so that additional lighting and appliance circuits can be added to the system. Home loan programs also may require that 60-amp service be updated before a home can qualify for financing.

To shut off power to a circuit, carefully unscrew the plug fuse, touching only its insulated rim. To shut off power to the entire house, hold the handle of the main fuse block and pull sharply to remove it. Major appliance circuits are controlled with another cartridge fuse block. Shut off the appliance circuit by pulling out this fuse block.

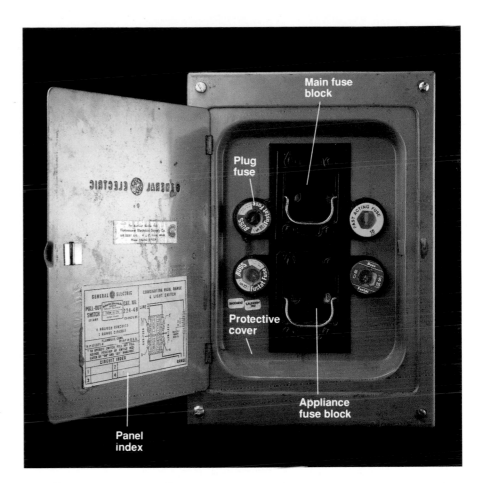

**A circuit breaker panel** providing 100 amps or more of power is common in wiring systems installed during the 1960s and later. A circuit breaker panel is housed in a gray metal cabinet that contains two rows of individual circuit breakers. The size of the service can be identified by reading the amperage rating of the main circuit breaker, which is located at the top of the main service panel.

A 100-amp service panel is now the minimum standard for most new housing. It is considered adequate for a medium-sized house with no more than three major electric appliances. However, larger houses with more electrical appliances require a service panel that provides 150 amps or more.

To shut off power to individual circuits in a circuit breaker panel, flip the lever on the appropriate circuit breaker to the OFF position. To shut off the power to the entire house, turn the main circuit breaker to the OFF position.

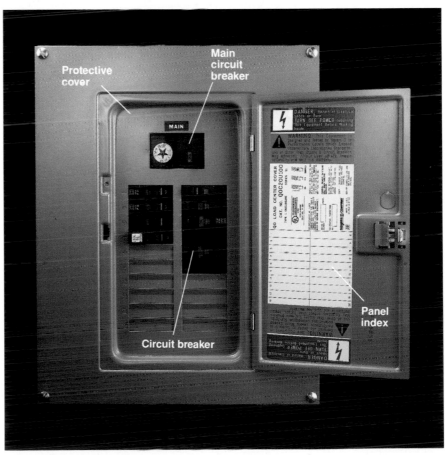

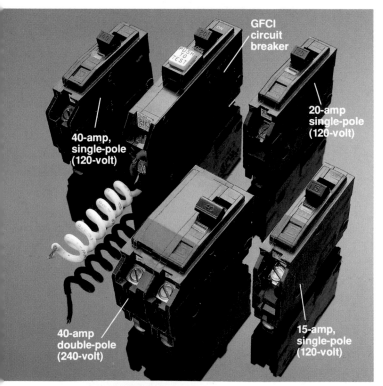

Cartridge
fuses

Time-delay
fuses

Regular
plug fuse

Regular
plug fuse

Tamper-proof
fuses

**Fuses** are used in older service panels. Plug fuses usually control 120-volt circuits rated for 15, 20 or 30 amps. Tamper-proof plug fuses have threads that fit only matching sockets, making it impossible to install a wrong-sized fuse. Time-delay fuses absorb temporary heavy power load without blowing. Cartridge fuses control 240-volt circuits and range from 30 to 100 amps.

GFCI
circuit
breaker

40-amp,
single-pole
(120-volt)

20-amp
single-pole
(120-volt)

40-amp
double-pole
(240-volt)

15-amp,
single-pole
(120-volt)

**Circuit breakers** are used in newer service panels. Single-pole breakers rated for 15 or 20 amps control 120-volt circuits. Double-pole breakers rated for 20 to 50 amps control 240-volt circuits. GFCI (ground-fault circuit-interrupter) breakers provide shock protection for the entire circuit.

# Fuses & Circuit Breakers

Fuses and circuit breakers are safety devices designed to protect the electrical system from short circuits and overloads. Fuses and circuit breakers are located in the main service panel.

Most service panels installed before 1965 rely on fuses to control and protect individual circuits. Screw-in plug fuses protect 120-volt circuits that power lights and receptacles. Cartridge fuses protect 240-volt appliance circuits and the main shutoff of the service panel.

Inside each fuse is a current-carrying metal alloy ribbon. If a circuit is overloaded, the metal ribbon melts and stops the flow of power. A fuse must match the amperage rating of the circuit. Never replace a fuse with one that has a larger amperage rating.

In most service panels installed after 1965, circuit breakers protect and control individual circuits. Single-pole circuit breakers protect 120-volt circuits, and double-pole circuit breakers protect 240-volt circuits. Amperage ratings for circuit breakers range from 15 to 100 amps.

Each circuit breaker has a permanent metal strip that heats up and bends when voltage passes through it. If a circuit is overloaded, the metal strip inside the breaker bends enough to "trip" the switch and stop the flow of power. If a circuit breaker trips frequently even though the power demand is small, the mechanism inside the breaker may be worn out. Worn circuit breakers should be replaced by an electrician.

When a fuse blows or a circuit breaker trips, it is usually because there are too many light fixtures and plug-in appliances drawing power through the circuit. Move some of the plug-in appliances to another circuit, then replace the fuse or reset the breaker. If the fuse blows or breaker trips again immediately, there may be a short circuit in the system. Call a licensed electrician if you suspect a short circuit.

**Everything You Need:**

Tools: fuse puller (for cartridge fuses only).

Materials: replacement fuse.

## How to Identify & Replace a Blown Plug Fuse

**1** Go to the main service panel and locate the blown fuse. If the metal ribbon inside fuse is cleanly melted (right), the circuit was overloaded. If window in fuse is discolored (left), there was a short circuit in the system.

**2** Unscrew the fuse, being careful to touch only the insulated rim of the fuse. Replace it with a fuse that has the same amperage rating.

## How to Remove, Test & Replace a Cartridge Fuse

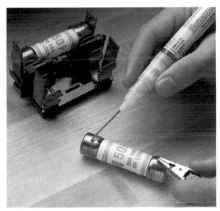

**1** Remove cartridge fuses by gripping the handle of the fuse block and pulling sharply.

**2** Remove the individual cartridge fuses from the block, using a fuse puller.

**3** Test each fuse, using a continuity tester. If the tester glows, the fuse is good. If the tester does not glow, replace the fuse with one that has the same amperage rating.

## How to Reset a Circuit Breaker

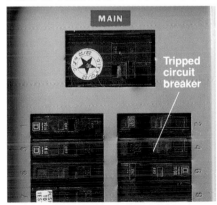

**1** Open the service panel and locate the tripped breaker. The lever on the tripped breaker will be either in the OFF position, or in a position between ON and OFF.

**2** Reset the tripped circuit breaker by pressing the circuit breaker lever all the way to the OFF position, then pressing it to the ON position.

**Test GFCI circuit breakers** by pushing TEST button. Breaker should trip to the OFF position. If not, the breaker is faulty and must be replaced by an electrician.

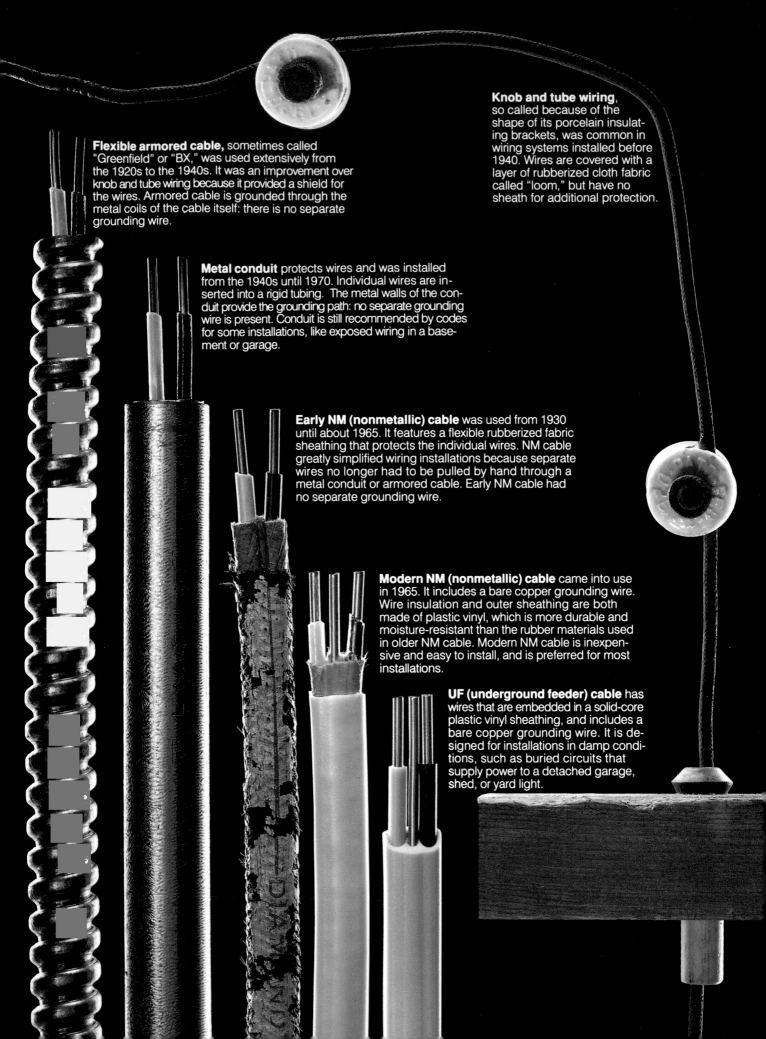

**Flexible armored cable,** sometimes called "Greenfield" or "BX," was used extensively from the 1920s to the 1940s. It was an improvement over knob and tube wiring because it provided a shield for the wires. Armored cable is grounded through the metal coils of the cable itself: there is no separate grounding wire.

**Knob and tube wiring,** so called because of the shape of its porcelain insulating brackets, was common in wiring systems installed before 1940. Wires are covered with a layer of rubberized cloth fabric called "loom," but have no sheath for additional protection.

**Metal conduit** protects wires and was installed from the 1940s until 1970. Individual wires are inserted into a rigid tubing. The metal walls of the conduit provide the grounding path: no separate grounding wire is present. Conduit is still recommended by codes for some installations, like exposed wiring in a basement or garage.

**Early NM (nonmetallic) cable** was used from 1930 until about 1965. It features a flexible rubberized fabric sheathing that protects the individual wires. NM cable greatly simplified wiring installations because separate wires no longer had to be pulled by hand through a metal conduit or armored cable. Early NM cable had no separate grounding wire.

**Modern NM (nonmetallic) cable** came into use in 1965. It includes a bare copper grounding wire. Wire insulation and outer sheathing are both made of plastic vinyl, which is more durable and moisture-resistant than the rubber materials used in older NM cable. Modern NM cable is inexpensive and easy to install, and is preferred for most installations.

**UF (underground feeder) cable** has wires that are embedded in a solid-core plastic vinyl sheathing, and includes a bare copper grounding wire. It is designed for installations in damp conditions, such as buried circuits that supply power to a detached garage, shed, or yard light.

# Wires & Cables

Wires are made of copper, aluminum, or aluminum covered with a thin layer of copper. Solid copper wires are the best conductors of electricity and are the most widely used. Aluminum and copper-covered aluminum wires require special installation techniques. They are discussed on page 98.

A group of two or more wires enclosed in a metal, rubber, or plastic sheath is called a **cable** (photo, page opposite). The sheath protects the wires from damage. Metal conduit also protects wires, but it is not considered a cable.

Individual wires are covered with rubber or plastic vinyl insulation. An exception is a bare copper grounding wire, which does not need an insulating cover. The insulation is color coded (chart, right) to identify the wire as a hot wire, a neutral wire, or a grounding wire.

In most wiring systems installed after 1965, the wires and cables are insulated with plastic vinyl. This type of insulation is very durable, and can last as long as the house itself.

Before 1965, wires and cables were insulated with rubber. Rubber insulation has a life expectancy of about 25 years. Old insulation that is cracked or damaged can be reinforced temporarily by wrapping the wire with plastic electrical tape. However, old wiring with cracked or damaged insulation should be inspected by a qualified electrician to make sure it is safe.

Wires must be large enough for the amperage rating of the circuit (chart, right). A wire that is too small can become dangerously hot. Wire sizes are categorized according to the American Wire Gauge (AWG) system. To check the size of a wire, use the wire stripper openings of a combination tool (page 84) as a guide.

| Wire color | | Function |
|---|---|---|
| | White | Neutral wire carrying current at zero voltage. |
| | Black | Hot wire carrying current at full voltage. |
| | Red | Hot wire carrying current at full voltage. |
| | White, black markings | Hot wire carrying current at full voltage. |
| | Green | Serves as a grounding pathway. |
| | Bare copper | Serves as a grounding pathway. |

**Individual wires are color coded** to identify their function. In some circuit installations, the white wire serves as a hot wire that carries voltage. If so, this white wire may be labeled with black tape or paint to identify it as a hot wire.

## Wire Size Chart

| Wire gauge | Wire capacity & use |
|---|---|
| #6 | 60 amps, 240 volts; central air conditioner, electric furnace. |
| #8 | 40 amps, 240 volts; electric range, central air conditioner. |
| #10 | 30 amps, 240 volts; window air conditioner, clothes dryer. |
| #12 | 20 amps, 120 volts; light fixtures, receptacles, microwave oven. |
| #14 | 15 amps, 120 volts; light fixtures, receptacles. |
| #16 | Light-duty extension cords. |
| #18 to 22 | Thermostats, doorbells, security systems. |

**Wire sizes** (shown actual size) are categorized by the American Wire Gauge system. The larger the wire size, the smaller the AWG number.

### Everything You Need:

Tools: cable ripper, combination tool, screwdriver, needlenose pliers.

Materials: wire nuts, pigtail wires (if needed).

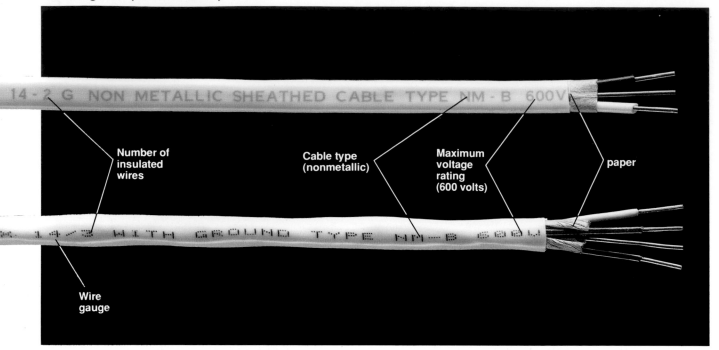

**Number of insulated wires**

**Cable type (nonmetallic)**

**Maximum voltage rating (600 volts)**

**paper**

**Wire gauge**

**NM (nonmetallic) cable is labeled** with the number of insulated wires it contains. The bare grounding wire is not counted. For example, a cable marked 14/2 G (or 14/2 WITH GROUND) contains two insulated 14-gauge wires, plus a bare copper grounding wire.

Cable marked 14/3 WITH GROUND has three 14-gauge wires plus a grounding wire. A strip of paper inside the cable protects the individual wires. NM cable also is stamped with a maximum voltage rating, as determined by Underwriters Laboratories (UL).

# Aluminum Wire

Inexpensive aluminum wire was used in place of copper in many wiring systems installed during the late 1960s and early 1970s, when copper prices were high. Aluminum wire is identified by its silver color,

and by the AL stamp on the cable sheathing. A variation, copper-clad aluminum wire, has a thin coating of copper bonded to a solid aluminum core.

By the early 1970s, all-aluminum wire was found to pose a safety hazard if connected to a switch or receptacle with brass or copper screw terminals. Because aluminum expands and contracts at a different rate than copper or brass, the wire connections could become loose. In some instances, fires resulted.

Existing aluminum wiring in homes is considered safe if proper installation methods have been followed, and if the wires are connected to special switches and receptacles designed to be used with aluminum wire. **If you have aluminum wire** in your home, have a qualified electrical inspector review the system. Copper-coated aluminum wire is not a hazard.

For a short while, switches and receptacles with an Underwriters Laboratories (UL) wire compatibility

rating of AL-CU were used with both aluminum and copper wiring. However, these devices proved to be hazardous when connected to aluminum wire. AL-CU devices should not be used with aluminum wiring.

In 1971, switches and receptacles designed for use with aluminum wiring were introduced. They are marked CO/ALR. This mark is now the only approved rating for aluminum wires. If your home has aluminum wires connected to a switch or receptacle without a CO/ALR rating stamp, replace the device with a switch or receptacle rated CO/ALR.

A switch or receptacle that has no wire compatibility rating printed on the mounting strap or casing should not be used with aluminum wires. These devices are designed for use with copper wires only.

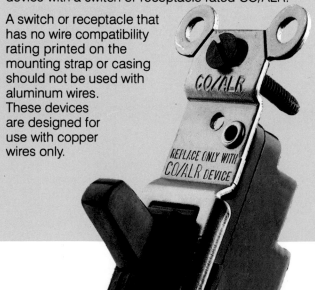

## How to Strip NM (Nonmetallic) Cable & Wires

**1** Measure and mark the cable 8" to 10" from end. Slide the cable ripper onto the cable, and squeeze tool firmly to force cutting point through plastic sheathing.

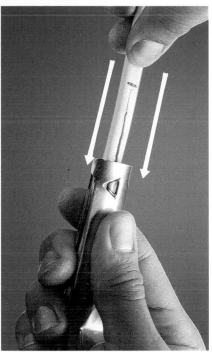

**2** Grip the cable tightly with one hand, and pull the cable ripper toward the end of the cable to cut open the plastic sheathing.

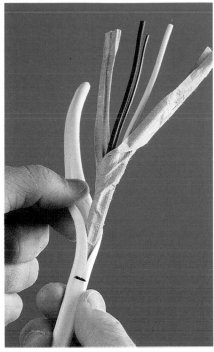

**3** Peel back the plastic sheathing and the paper wrapping from the individual wires.

**4** Cut away the excess plastic sheathing and paper wrapping, using the cutting jaws of a combination tool.

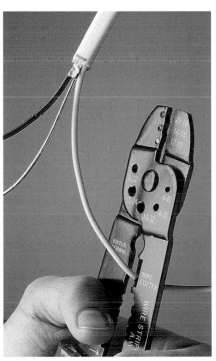

**5** Cut the individual wires, if necessary, using the cutting jaws of the combination tool.

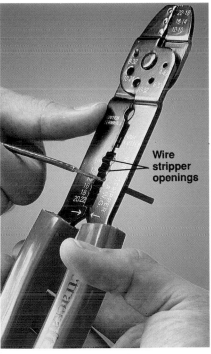

**6** Strip insulation from each wire, using the stripper openings. Choose the opening that matches the gauge of the wire, and take care not to nick or scratch the ends of the wires.

## How to Connect Wires to Screw Terminals

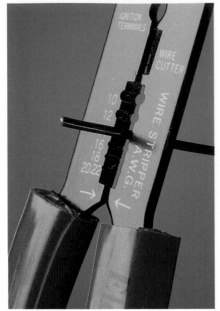 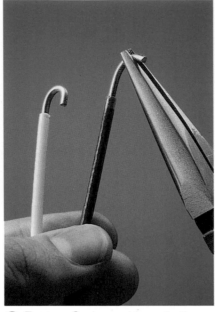 

**1** Strip about ¾" of insulation from each wire, using a combination tool. Choose the stripper opening that matches the gauge of the wire, then clamp wire in tool. Pull the wire firmly to remove plastic insulation.

**2** Form a C-shaped loop in the end of each wire, using a needlenose pliers. The wire should have no scratches or nicks.

**3** Hook each wire around the screw terminal so it forms a clockwise loop. Tighten screw firmly. Insulation should just touch head of screw. Never place the ends of two wires under a single screw terminal. Instead, use a pigtail wire (page opposite).

## How to Connect Wires with Push-in Fittings

  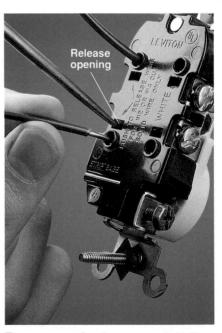

**1** Mark the amount of insulation to be stripped from each wire, using the strip gauge on the back of the switch or receptacle. Strip the wires using a combination tool (step 1, above). Never use push-in fittings with aluminum wiring.

**2** Insert the bare copper wires firmly into the push-in fittings on the back of the switch or receptacle. When inserted, wires should have no bare copper exposed.

**Remove a wire** from a push-in fitting by inserting a small nail or screwdriver in the release opening next to the wire. Wire will pull out easily.

## How to Connect Two or More Wires with a Wire Nut

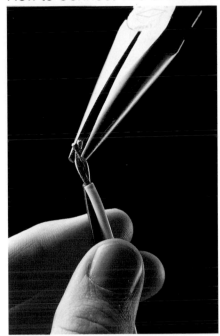

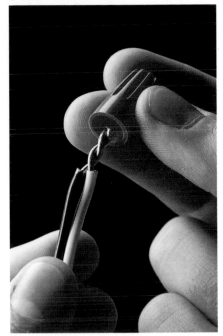

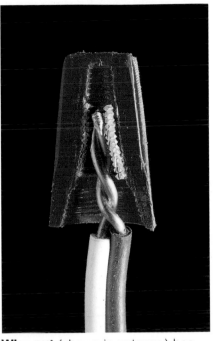

**1** Strip about ½" of insulation from each wire. Hold the wires parallel, and twist them together in a clockwise direction, using a needle-nose pliers or combination tool.

**2** Screw the wire nut onto the twisted wires. Tug gently on each wire to make sure it is secure. In a proper connection, no bare wire should be exposed past the bottom of the wire nut.

**Wire nut** (shown in cutaway) has metal threads that grip the bare ends of the wires. When connected, the wire nut should completely cover the bare wires.

## How to Pigtail Two or More Wires

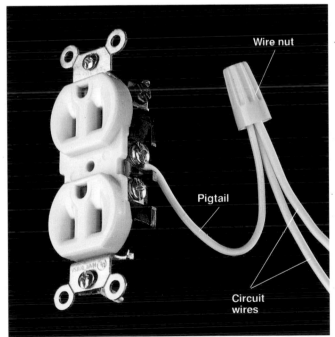

Wire nut

Pigtail

Circuit wires

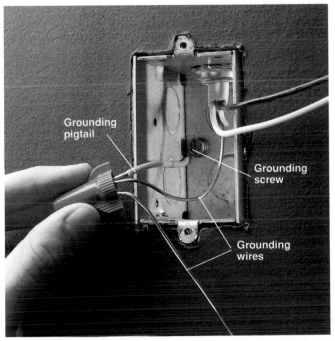

Grounding pigtail

Grounding screw

Grounding wires

**Connect two or more wires** to a single screw terminal with a pigtail. A pigtail is a short piece of wire. One end of the pigtail connects to a screw terminal and the other end connects to circuit wires, using a wire nut. A pigtail also can be used to lengthen circuit wires that are too short.

**Grounding pigtail** has green insulation, and is available with a preattached grounding screw. This grounding screw connects to the grounded metal electrical box. The end of the pigtail wire connects to the bare copper grounding wires with a wire nut.

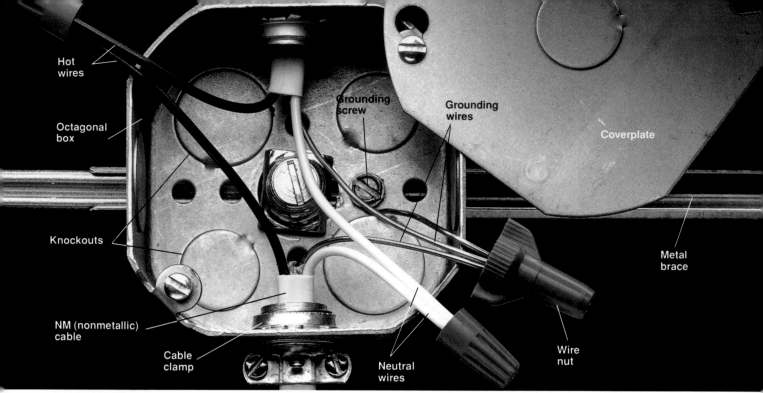

Hot wires

Octagonal box

Knockouts

NM (nonmetallic) cable

Cable clamp

Grounding screw

Grounding wires

Coverplate

Metal brace

Neutral wires

Wire nut

**Octagonal boxes** usually contain wire connections for ceiling fixtures. Cables are inserted into the box through knockout openings, and are held with cable clamps. Because the ceiling fixture attaches directly to the box, the box should be anchored firmly to a framing member. Often, it is nailed directly to a ceiling joist. However, metal braces are available that allow a box to be mounted between joists or studs. A properly installed octagonal box can support a ceiling fixture weighing up to 35 pounds. Any box must be covered with a tightly fitting coverplate, and the box must not have open knockouts.

# Electrical Boxes

The National Electrical Code requires that wire connections or cable splices be contained inside an approved metal or plastic box. This shields framing members and other flammable materials from electrical sparks. If you have exposed wire connections or cable splices, protect your home by installing electrical boxes.

Electrical boxes come in several shapes. Rectangular and square boxes are used for switches and receptacles. Rectangular (2" × 3") boxes are used for single switches or duplex receptacles. Square (4" × 4") boxes are used anytime it is convenient for two switches or receptacles to be wired or "ganged" in one box, an arrangement common in kitchens or entry hallways. Octagonal electrical boxes contain wire connections for ceiling fixtures.

All electrical boxes are available in different depths. A box must be deep enough so a switch or receptacle can be removed or installed easily without crimping and damaging the circuit wires. Replace an undersized box with a larger box, using the Electrical Box Chart (right) as a guide. The NEC also says that all electrical boxes must remain accessible. Never cover an electrical box with drywall, paneling, or wallcoverings.

## Electrical Box Chart

| Box Shape | | Maximum number of individual wires in box* | |
|---|---|---|---|
| | | 14-gauge | 12-gauge |
| 2" × 3" rectangular | 2½" deep | 3 | 3 |
| | 3½" deep | 5 | 4 |
| 4" × 4" square | 1½" deep | 6 | 5 |
| | 2⅛" deep | 9 | 7 |
| Octagonal | 1½" deep | 4 | 3 |
| | 2⅛" deep | 7 | 6 |

* Do not count pigtail wires or grounding wires.

# Common Electrical Boxes

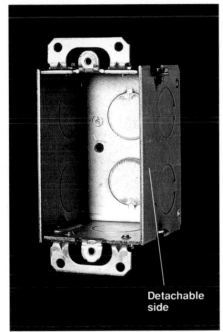

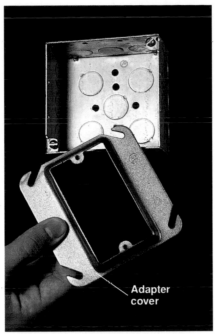

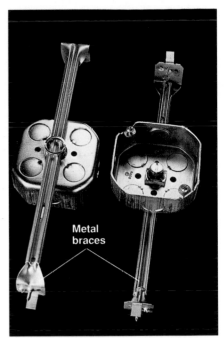

Detachable side

Adapter cover

Metal braces

**Rectangular boxes** are used with wall switches and duplex receptacles. Single-size rectangular boxes (shown above) may have detachable sides that allow them to be ganged together to form double-size boxes.

**Square 4" × 4" boxes** are large enough for most wiring applications. They are used for cable splices and ganged receptacles or switches. To install one switch or receptacle in a square box, use an adapter cover.

**Braced octagonal boxes** fit between ceiling joists. The metal braces extend to fit any joist spacing, and are nailed or screwed to framing members.

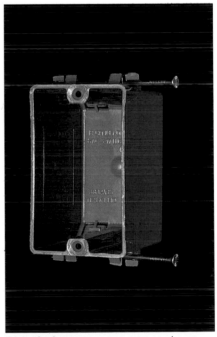

Foam gasket

Built-in clamp

**Outdoor boxes** have sealed seams and foam gaskets to guard a switch or receptacle against moisture. Corrosion-resistant coatings protect all metal parts.

**Retrofit boxes** upgrade older boxes to larger sizes. One type (above) has built-in clamps that tighten against the inside of a wall and hold the box in place. A retrofit box with flexible brackets is shown on pages 106 to 107.

**Plastic boxes** are common in new construction. They can be used only with NM (nonmetallic) cable. Box may include preattached nails for anchoring the box to framing members.

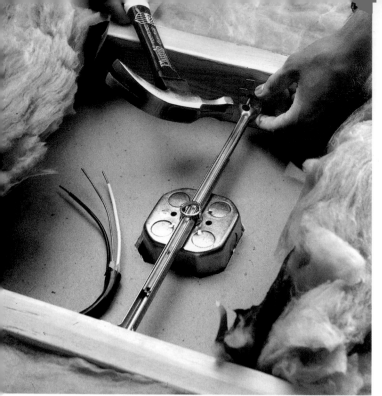

**Electrical boxes** are required for all wire connections. The box protects wood and other flammable materials from electrical sparks (arcing). Electrical boxes should always be anchored to joists or studs.

# Installing an Electrical Box

Install an electrical box any time you find exposed wire connections or cable splices. Exposed connections sometimes can be found in older homes, where wires attach to light fixtures. Exposed splices can be found in areas where NM (nonmetallic) cable runs through uncovered joists or wall studs, such as in an unfinished basement or utility room.

When installing an electrical box, make sure there is enough cable to provide about 8" of wire inside the box. If the wires are too short, you can add pigtails to lengthen them. If the electrical box is metal, make sure the circuit grounding wires are pigtailed to the box.

**Everything You Need:**

Tools: neon circuit tester, screwdriver, hammer, combination tool.

Materials: screws or nails, electrical box, cable connectors, pigtail wire, wire nuts.

## How to Install an Electrical Box for Cable Splices

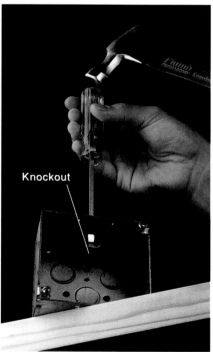

Knockout

**1** Turn off power to circuit wires at the main service panel. Carefully remove any tape or wire nuts from the exposed splice. Avoid contact with the bare wire ends until the wires have been tested for power.

**2** Test for power. Touch one probe of a circuit tester to the black hot wires, and touch other probe to the white neutral wires. The tester should not glow. If it does, the wires are still hot. Shut off power to correct circuit at the main service panel. Disconnect the splice wires.

**3** Open one knockout for each cable that will enter the box, using a hammer and screwdriver. Any unopened knockouts should remain sealed.

**4** Anchor the electrical box to a wooden framing member, using screws or nails.

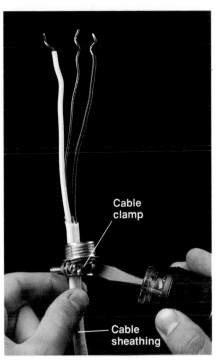

**5** Thread each cable through a cable clamp. Tighten the clamp with a screwdriver. Do not overtighten. Overtightening can damage cable sheathing.

Cable clamp

Cable sheathing

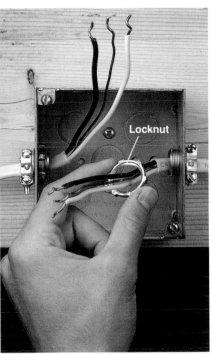

**6** Insert the cables into the electrical box, and screw a locknut onto each cable clamp.

Locknut

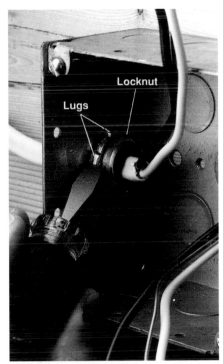

**7** Tighten the locknuts by pushing against the lugs with the blade of a screwdriver.

Locknut

Lugs

**8** Use wire nuts to reconnect the wires. Pigtail the copper grounding wires to the green grounding screw in the back of the box.

Grounding screw

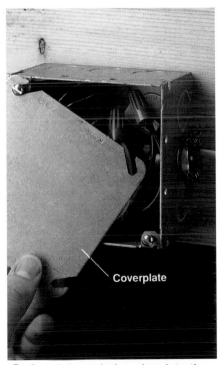

**9** Carefully tuck the wires into the box, and attach the coverplate. Turn on the power to the circuit at the main service panel. Make sure the box remains accessible, and is not covered with finished walls or ceilings.

Coverplate

# Replacing an Electrical Box

Replace any electrical box that is too small for the number of wires it contains. Forcing wires into an undersized box can damage wires, disturb wire connections, and create a potential fire hazard.

Boxes that are too small often are found when repairing or replacing switches, receptacles, or light fixtures. If you find a box so small that you have difficulty fitting the wires inside, replace it with a larger box. Use the chart on page 102 as a guide when choosing a replacement box.

Metal and plastic retrofit electrical boxes are available in a variety of styles, and can be purchased at any hardware store or home center. Most can be installed without damaging the wall surfaces.

## Everything You Need:

Tools: screwdriver, neon circuit tester, reciprocating saw, hammer, needlenose pliers.

Materials: electrical tape, retrofit electrical box with flexible brackets, grounding screw.

## How to Replace an Electrical Box

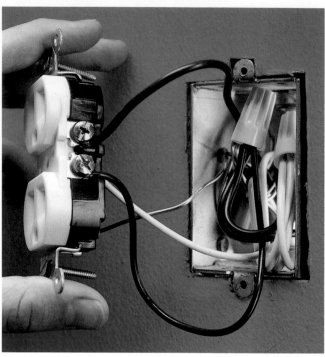

**1** Shut off the power to the circuit at the main service panel. Test for power with a neon circuit tester (switches, page 115; receptacles, page 120; light fixtures, page 126). Disconnect and remove receptacle switch, or fixture from the existing box.

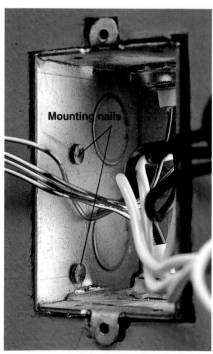

**2** Examine the box to determine how it was installed. Most older metal boxes are attached to framing members with nails, and the nail heads will be visible inside the box.

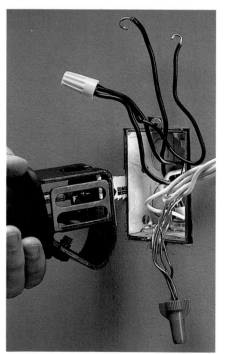

**3** Cut through the mounting nails by slipping the metal-cutting blade of a reciprocating saw between the box and framing member. Take care not to damage the circuit wires. Disconnect wires.

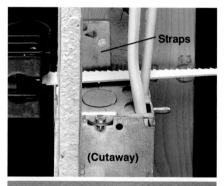

**If box is mounted with straps** (shown with wall cut away) remove the box by cutting through the straps, using a reciprocating saw and metal-cutting blade. Take care not to damage the wires.

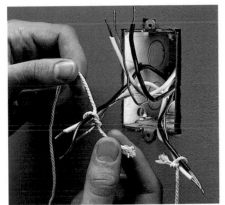

**4** To prevent wires from falling into wall cavity, gather wires from each cable and tie them together, using pieces of string.

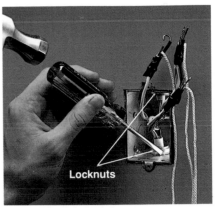

**5** Secure the string to the wires, using a piece of plastic electrical tape.

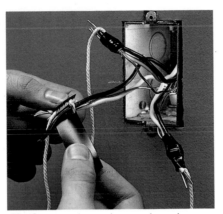

**6** Disconnect the internal clamps or locknuts that hold the circuit cables to the box.

Locknuts

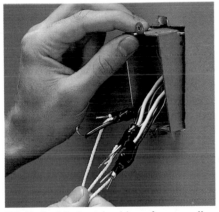

**7** Pull old electrical box from wall. Take care not to damage insulation on circuit wires, and hold on to string to make sure wires do not fall inside wall cavity.

**8** Tape the wires to the edge of the wall cutout.

**9** Punch out one knockout for each cable that will enter the new electrical box, using a screwdriver and hammer.

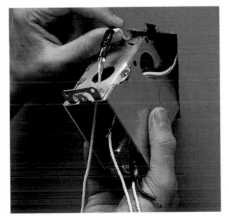

**10** Thread cables into the new electrical box, and slide the box into the wall opening. Tighten the internal clamps or locknuts holding the circuit cables to the electrical box. Remove the strings.

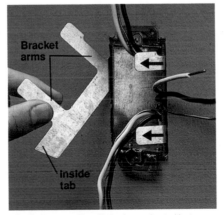

Bracket arms

inside tab

**11** Insert flexible brackets into the wall on each side of the electrical box. Pull out bracket arms until inside tab is tight against inside of the wall.

Bracket arms

**12** Bend bracket arms around walls of box, using needlenose pliers. Reinstall the fixture, and turn on the power to the circuit at the main service panel.

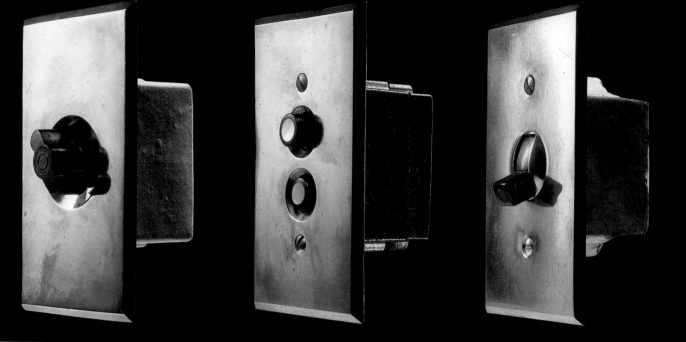

**Rotary snap switches** are found in many installations completed between 1900 and 1920. Handle is twisted clockwise to turn light on and off. The switch is enclosed in a ceramic housing.

**Push-button switches** were widely used from 1920 until about 1940. Many switches of this type are still in operation. Reproductions of this switch type are available for restoration projects.

**Toggle switches** were introduced in the 1930s. This early design has a switch mechanism that is mounted in a ceramic housing sealed with a layer of insulating paper.

# Common Wall-switch Problems

An average wall switch is turned on and off more than 1,000 times each year. Because switches receive constant use, wire connections can loosen and switch parts gradually wear out. If a switch no longer operates smoothly, it must be repaired or replaced.

The methods for repairing or replacing a switch vary slightly, depending on the switch type and its location along an electrical circuit. Individual switch styles may vary from manufacturer to manufacturer, but the basic switch types are universal.

It is possible to replace most ordinary wall switches with a specialty switch, like a timer switch or an electronic switch. When installing a specialty switch, make sure it is compatible with the wiring configuration of the switch box.

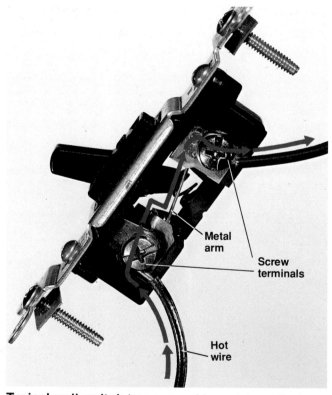

Metal arm

Screw terminals

Hot wire

**Typical wall switch** has a movable metal arm that opens and closes the electrical circuit. When the switch is ON, the arm completes the circuit and power flows between the screw terminals and through the black hot wire to the light fixture. When the switch is OFF, the arm lifts away to interrupt the circuit, and no power flows. Switch problems can occur if the screw terminals are not tight, or if the metal arm inside the switch wears out.

**Toggle switches** were improved during the 1950s, and are now the most commonly used type. This switch type was the first to use a sealed plastic housing that protects the inner switch mechanism from dust and moisture.

**Mercury switches** became common in the early 1960s. They conduct electrical current by means of a sealed vial of mercury. Although more expensive than other types, mercury switches are durable: some are guaranteed for 50 years.

**Electronic motion-sensor switch** has an infrared eye that senses movement and automatically turns on lights when a person enters a room. Motion-sensor switches can provide added security against intruders.

| Problem | Repair |
|---|---|
| Fuse burns out or circuit breaker trips when the switch is turned on. | 1. Tighten any loose wire connections on switch (pages 114 to 115). 2. Move lamps or plug-in appliances to other circuits to prevent overloads. 3. Test switch (pages 110 to 113), and replace, if needed (pages 114 to 117). 4. Repair or replace faulty fixture (pages 124 to 139) or faulty appliance. |
| Light fixture or permanently installed appliance does not work. | 1. Replace burned-out light bulb. 2. Check for blown fuse or tripped circuit breaker to make sure circuit is operating (pages 94 to 95). 3. Check for loose wire connections on switch (pages 114 to 115). 4. Test switch (pages 110 to 113), and replace (pages 114 to 117). 5. Repair or replace light fixture (pages 124 to 139) or appliance. |
| Light fixture flickers. | 1. Tighten light bulb in the socket. 2. Check for loose wire connections on switch (pages 114 to 115). 3. Repair or replace light fixture (pages 124 to 139), or switch (pages 114 to 117). |
| Switch buzzes or is warm to the touch. | 1. Check for loose wire connections on switch (pages 114 to 115). 2. Test switch (pages 110 to 113), and replace, if needed (pages 114 to 117). 3. Move lamps or appliances to other circuits to reduce demand. |
| Switch lever does not stay in position. | Replace worn-out switch (pages 114 to 117). |

# Testing Switches for Continuity

A switch that does not work properly may have worn or broken internal parts. Test for internal wear with a battery-operated continuity tester. The continuity tester detects any break in the metal pathway inside the switch. Replace the switch if the continuity tester shows the switch to be faulty.

Never use a continuity tester on wires that might carry live current. Always shut off the power and disconnect the switch before testing for continuity.

Some specialty switches, like dimmers, cannot be tested for continuity. Electronic switches can be tested for manual operation using a continuity tester, but the automatic operation of these switches cannot be tested.

**Everything You Need:**

Tools: continuity tester.

## How to Test a Single-pole Wall Switch

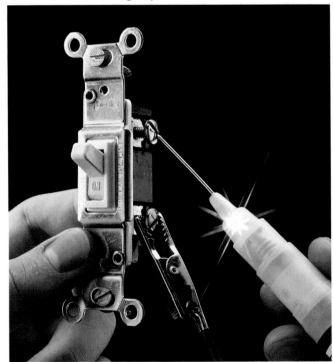

**Attach clip** of tester to one of the screw terminals. Touch the tester probe to the other screw terminal. Flip switch lever from ON to OFF. If switch is good, tester glows when lever is ON, but not when OFF.

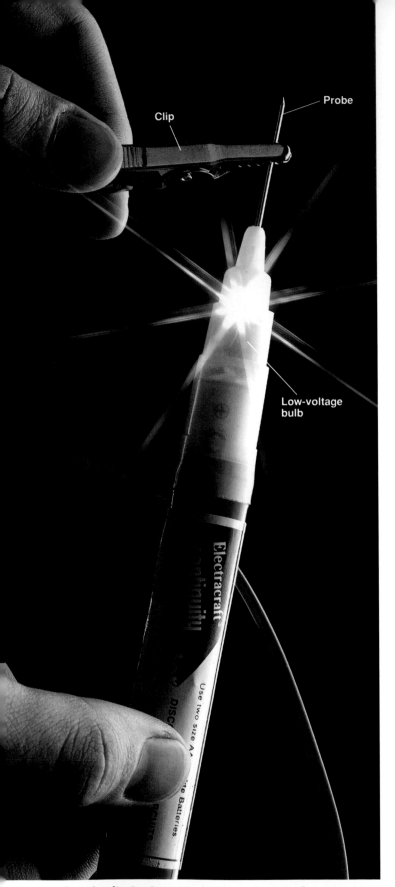

Clip

Probe

Low-voltage bulb

**Continuity tester** uses battery-generated current to test the metal pathways running through switches and other electrical fixtures. Always "test" the tester before use. Touch the tester clip to the metal probe. The tester should glow. If not, then the battery or light bulb is dead and must be replaced.

## How to Test a Three-way Wall Switch

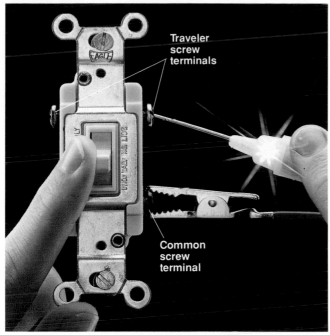

Traveler screw terminals

Common screw terminal

**1** Attach tester clip to the dark common screw terminal. Touch the tester probe to one of the traveler screw terminals, and flip switch lever back and forth. If switch is good, the tester should glow when the lever is in one position, but not both.

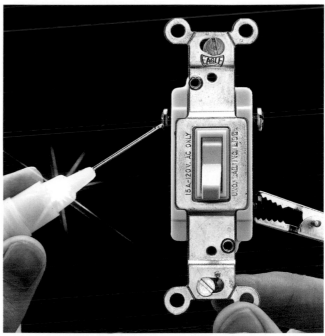

**2** Touch probe to the other traveler screw terminal, and flip the switch lever back and forth. If switch is good, the tester will glow only when the switch lever is in the position opposite from the positive test in step 1.

## How to Test a Four-way Wall Switch

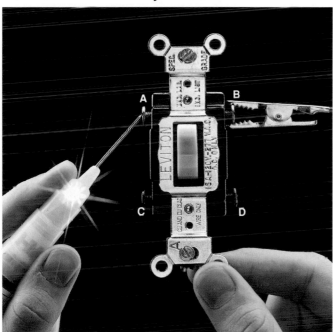

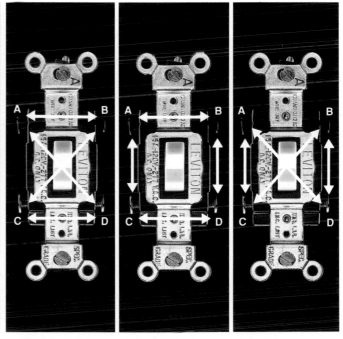

**1** Test switch by touching probe and clip of continuity tester to each pair of screw terminals (A-B, C-D, A-D, B-C, A-C, B-D). The test should show continuous pathways between two different pairs of screw terminals. Flip lever to opposite position, and repeat test. Test should show continuous pathways between two different pairs of screw terminals.

**2** If switch is good, test will show a total of four continuous pathways between screw terminals — two pathways for each lever position. If not, then switch is faulty and must be replaced. (The arrangement of the pathways may differ, depending on the switch manufacturer. The photo above shows the three possible pathway arrangements.)

## How to Test a Pilot-light Switch

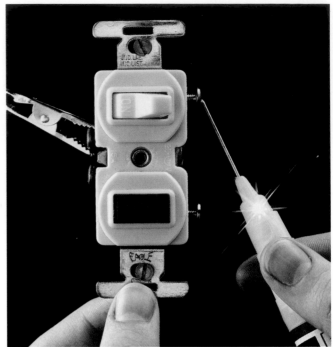

**1** Test pilot light by flipping the switch lever to the ON position. Check to see if the light fixture or appliance is working. If the pilot light does not glow even though the switch operates the light fixture or appliance, then the pilot light is defective and the unit must be replaced.

**2** Test the switch by disconnecting the unit. With the switch lever in the ON position, attach the tester clip to the top screw terminal on one side of the switch. Touch tester probe to top screw terminal on opposite side of the switch. If switch is good, tester will glow when switch is ON, but not when OFF.

## How to Test a Timer Switch

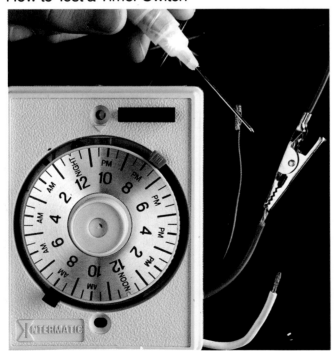

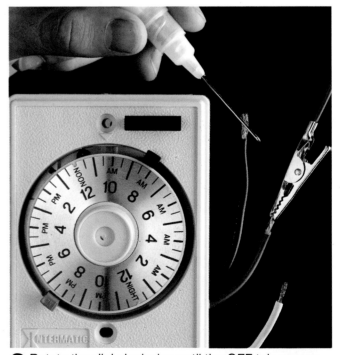

**1** Attach the tester clip to the red wire lead on the timer switch, and touch the tester probe to the black hot lead. Rotate the timer dial clockwise until the ON tab passes the arrow marker. Tester should glow. If it does not, the switch is faulty and must be replaced.

**2** Rotate the dial clockwise until the OFF tab passes the arrow marker. Tester should not glow. If it does, the switch is faulty and must be replaced.

## How to Test Switch/receptacle

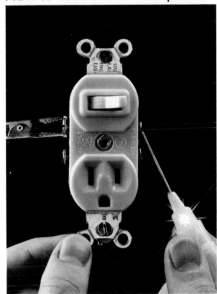

**Attach tester clip** to one of the top screw terminals. Touch the tester probe to the top screw terminal on the opposite side. Flip the switch lever from ON to OFF position. If the switch is working correctly, the tester will glow when the switch lever is ON, but not when OFF.

## How to Test a Double Switch

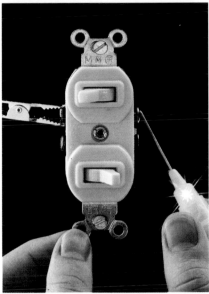

**Test each half of switch** by attaching the tester clip to one screw terminal, and touching the probe to the opposite side. Flip switch lever from ON to OFF position. If switch is good, tester glows when the switch lever is ON, but not when OFF. Repeat test with the remaining pair of screw terminals. If either half tests faulty, replace the unit.

## How to Test a Time-delay Switch

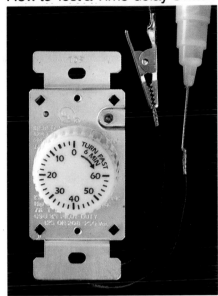

**Attach tester clip** to one of the wire leads, and touch the tester probe to the other lead. Set the timer for a few minutes. If switch is working correctly, the tester will glow until the time expires.

## How to Test Manual Operation of Electronic Switches

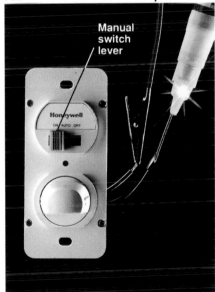

**Automatic switch:** Attach the tester clip to a black wire lead, and touch the tester probe to the other black lead. Flip the manual switch lever from ON to OFF position. If switch is working correctly, tester will glow when the switch lever is ON, but not when OFF.

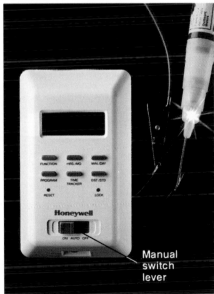

**Programmable switch:** Attach the tester clip to a wire lead, and touch the tester probe to the other lead. Flip the manual switch lever from ON to OFF position. If the switch is working correctly, the tester will glow when the switch lever is ON, but not when OFF.

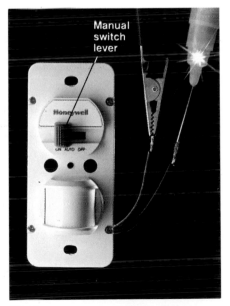

**Motion-sensor switch:** Attach the tester clip to a wire lead, and touch the tester probe to the other lead. Flip the manual switch lever from ON to OFF position. If the switch is working correctly, the tester will glow when the switch lever is ON, but not when OFF.

# Fixing & Replacing Wall Switches

Most switch problems are caused by loose wire connections. If a fuse blows or a circuit breaker trips when a switch is turned on, a loose wire may be touching the metal box. Loose wires also can cause switches to overheat or buzz.

Switches sometimes fail because internal parts wear out. To check for wear, the switch must be removed entirely and tested for continuity (pages 110 to 113). If the continuity test shows the switch is faulty, replace it.

## Everything You Need:

Tools: screwdriver, neon circuit tester, continuity tester, combination tool.

Materials: fine sandpaper, anti-oxidant paste (for aluminum wiring).

## How to Fix or Replace a Single-pole Wall Switch

**1** Turn off the power to the switch at the main service panel, then remove the switch coverplate.

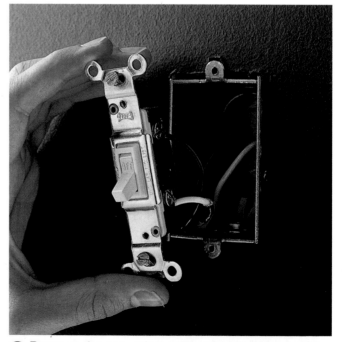

**2** Remove the mounting screws holding the switch to the electrical box. Holding the mounting straps carefully, pull the switch from the box. Be careful not to touch any bare wires or screw terminals until the switch has been tested for power.

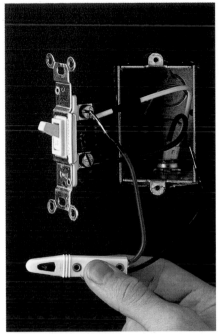

**3** Test for power by touching one probe of the neon circuit tester to the grounded metal box or to the bare copper grounding wire, and touching other probe to each screw terminal. Tester should not glow. If it does, there is still power entering the box. Return to service panel and turn off correct circuit.

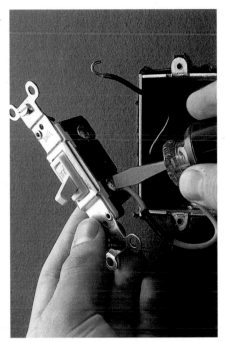

**4** Disconnect the circuit wires and remove the switch. Test the switch for continuity (page 110), and buy a replacement if the switch is faulty. If circuit wires are too short, lengthen them by adding pigtail wires.

**5** If wires are broken or nicked, clip off damaged portion, using a combination tool. Strip wires so there is about ¾" of bare wire at the end of each wire.

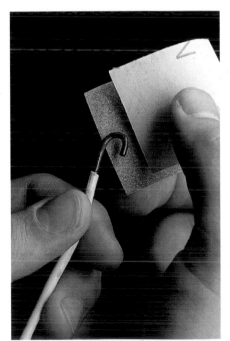

**6** Clean the bare copper wires with fine sandpaper if they appear darkened or dirty. If wires are aluminum, apply an anti-oxidant paste before connecting the wires.

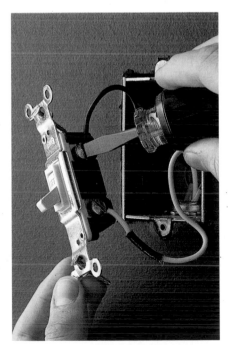

**7** Connect the wires to the screw terminals on the switch. Tighten the screws firmly, but do not overtighten. Overtightening may strip the screw threads.

**8** Remount the switch, carefully tucking the wires inside the box. Reattach the switch coverplate and turn on the power to the switch at the main service panel.

## How to Fix or Replace a Three-way Wall Switch

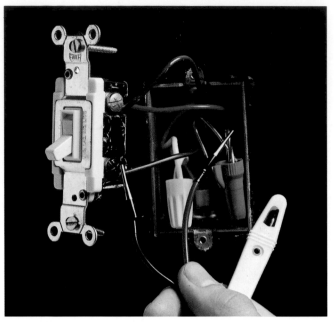

**1** Turn off power to the switch at the main service panel, then remove the switch coverplate and mounting screws. Holding the mounting strap carefully, pull the switch from the box. Be careful not to touch the bare wires or screw terminals until they have been tested for power.

**2** Test for power by touching one probe of the neon circuit tester to the grounded metal box or to the bare copper grounding wire, and touching the other probe to each screw terminal. Tester should not glow. If it does, there is still power entering the box. Return to the service panel and turn off the correct circuit.

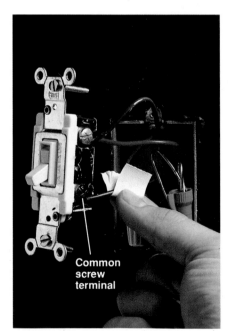

Common screw terminal

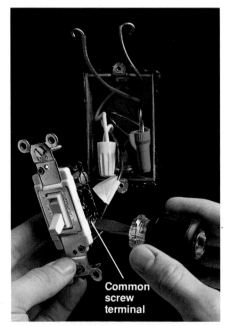

Common screw terminal

**3** Locate dark common screw terminal, and use masking tape to label the "common" wire attached to it. Disconnect wires and remove switch. Test switch for continuity (page 111). If it tests faulty, buy a replacement. Inspect wires for nicks and scratches. If necessary, clip damaged wires and strip them (page 99).

**4** Connect the common wire to the dark common screw terminal on the switch. On most three-way switches the common screw terminal is copper. Or, it may be labeled with the word COMMON stamped on the back of the switch.

**5** Connect the remaining wires to the brass or silver screw terminals. These wires are interchangeable, and can be connected to either screw terminal. Carefully tuck the wires into the box. Remount the switch, and attach the coverplate. Turn on the power at the main service panel.

## How to Fix or Replace a Four-way Wall Switch

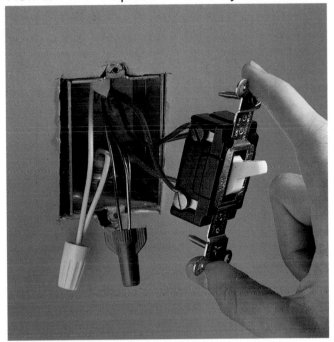

**1** Turn off the power to the switch at the main service panel, then remove the switch coverplate and mounting screws. Holding the mounting strap carefully, pull the switch from the box. Be careful not to touch any bare wires or screw terminals until they have been tested for power.

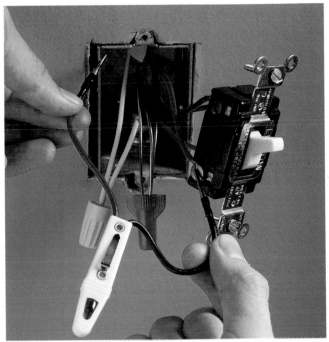

**2** Test for power by touching one probe of the circuit tester to the grounded metal box or bare copper grounding wire, and touching the other probe to each of the screw terminals. Tester should not glow. If it does, there is still power entering the box. Return to the service panel and turn off the correct circuit.

**3** Disconnect the wires and inspect them for nicks and scratches. If necessary, clip damaged wires and strip them (page 99). Test the switch for continuity (page 111). Buy a replacement if the switch tests faulty.

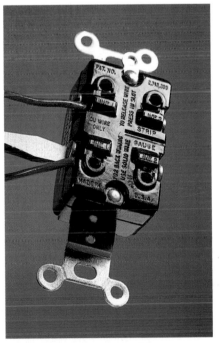

**4** Connect two wires of the same color to the brass screw terminals. On the switch shown above, the brass screw terminals are labeled LINE 1.

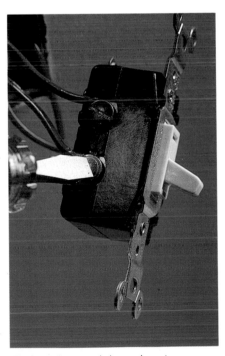

**5** Attach remaining wires to copper screw terminals, marked LINE 2 on some switches. Carefully tuck the wires inside the switch box, then remount the switch and attach the coverplate. Turn on the power at the main service panel.

The earliest receptacles were modifications of the screw-in type light bulb. This receptacle was used in the early 1900s.

# Common Receptacle Problems

Household receptacles, also called outlets, have no moving parts to wear out, and usually last for many years without servicing. Most problems associated with receptacles are actually caused by faulty lamps and appliances, or their plugs and cords. However, the constant plugging in and removal of appliance cords can wear out the metal contacts inside a receptacle. Any receptacle that does not hold plugs firmly should be replaced.

A loose wire connection is another possible problem. A loose connection can spark (called arcing), trip a circuit breaker, or cause heat to build up in the receptacle box, creating a potential fire hazard.

Wires can come loose for a number of reasons. Everyday vibrations caused by walking across floors, or from nearby street traffic, may cause a connection to shake loose. In addition, because wires heat and cool with normal use, the ends of the wires will expand and contract slightly. This movement also may cause the wires to come loose from the screw terminal connections.

The polarized receptacle became standard in the 1920s. The different sized slots direct current flow for safety.

The ground-fault circuit-interrupter, or GFCI receptacle, is a modern safety device. When it detects slight changes in current, it instantly shuts off power.

| Problem | Repair |
|---|---|
| Circuit breaker trips repeatedly, or fuse burns out immediately after being replaced. | 1. Repair or replace worn or damaged lamp or appliance cord.<br>2. Move lamps or appliances to other circuits to prevent overloads.<br>3. Tighten any loose wire connections (pages 122 to 123).<br>4. Clean dirty or oxidized wire ends (page 122). |
| Lamp or appliance does not work. | 1. Make sure lamp or appliance is plugged in.<br>2. Replace burned-out bulbs.<br>3. Repair or replace worn or damaged lamp or appliance cord.<br>4. Tighten any loose wire connections (pages 122 to 123).<br>5. Clean dirty or oxidized wire ends (page 122).<br>6. Repair or replace any faulty receptacle (pages 122 to 123). |
| Receptacle does not hold plugs firmly. | 1. Repair or replace worn or damaged plugs (pages 142 to 143).<br>2. Replace faulty receptacles (pages 122 to 123). |
| Receptacle is warm to the touch, buzzes, or sparks when plugs are inserted or removed. | 1. Move lamps or appliances to other circuits to prevent overloads.<br>2. Tighten any loose wire connections (pages 122 to 123).<br>3. Clean dirty or oxidized wire ends (page 122).<br>4. Replace faulty receptacles (pages 122 to 123). |

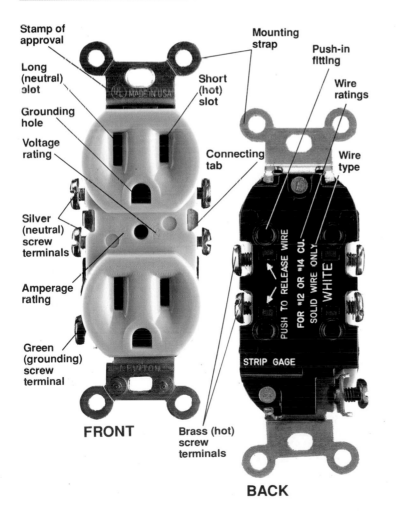

Stamp of approval

Long (neutral) slot

Grounding hole

Voltage rating

Silver (neutral) screw terminals

Amperage rating

Green (grounding) screw terminal

**FRONT**

Mounting strap

Short (hot) slot

Connecting tab

Push-in fitting

Wire ratings

Wire type

Brass (hot) screw terminals

**BACK**

**The standard duplex receptacle** has two halves for receiving plugs. Each half has a long (neutral) slot, a short (hot) slot, and a U-shaped grounding hole. The slots fit the wide prong, narrow prong, and grounding prong of a three-prong plug. This ensures that the connection between receptacle and plug will be polarized and grounded for safety (page 82).

Wires are attached to the receptacle at screw terminals or push-in fittings. A connecting tab between the screw terminals allows a variety of different wiring configurations. Receptacles also include mounting straps for attaching to electrical boxes.

Stamps of approval from testing agencies are found on the front and back of the receptacle. Look for the symbol UL or UND. LAB. INC. LIST to make sure the receptacle meets the strict standards of Underwriters Laboratories.

The receptacle is marked with ratings for maximum volts and amps. The common receptacle is marked 15A, 125V. Receptacles marked CU or COPPER are used with solid copper wire. Those marked CU-CLAD ONLY are used with copper-coated aluminum wire. Only receptacles marked CO/ALR may be used with solid aluminum wiring (page 98). Receptacles marked AL/CU no longer may be used with aluminum wire according to code.

**Metal probes**

**Insulated handles**

**Bulb**

# Testing Receptacles for Power, Grounding & Polarity

**Test for power** to make sure that live voltage is not reaching the receptacle during a repair or replacement project.

**Test for grounding** to plan receptacle replacements. The test for grounding will indicate how an existing receptacle is wired, and whether a replacement receptacle should be a two-slot polarized receptacle, a grounded three-slot receptacle, or a GFCI.

If the test indicates that the hot and neutral wires are reversed, make sure the wires are installed correctly on the replacement receptacle.

**Test for hot wires** if you need to confirm which wire is carrying live voltage.

An inexpensive neon circuit tester makes it easy to perform these tests. It has a small bulb that glows when electrical power flows through it.

Remember that the tester only glows when it is part of a complete circuit. For example, if you touch one probe to a hot wire and do not touch anything with the other probe, the tester will not glow, even though the hot wire is carrying power. When using the tester, take care not to touch the metal probes.

When testing for power or grounding, always confirm any negative (tester does not glow) results by removing the coverplate and examining the receptacle to make sure all wires are intact and properly connected. Do not touch any wires without first turning off the power at the main service panel.

### Everything You Need:

Tools: neon circuit tester, screwdriver.

## How to Test a Receptacle for Power

**1** Turn off power at the main service panel. Place one probe of the tester in each slot of the receptacle. The tester should not glow. If it does glow, the correct circuit has not been turned off at the main service panel. Test both ends of a duplex receptacle. Remember that this is a preliminary test. You must confirm that power is off by removing the coverplate and testing for power at the receptacle wires (step 2).

**2** Remove the receptacle coverplate. Loosen the mounting screws and carefully pull the receptacle from its box. Take care not to touch any wires. Touch one probe of the neon tester to a brass screw terminal, and one probe to a silver screw terminal. The tester should not glow. If it does, you must shut off the correct circuit at the service panel. If wires are connected to both sets of terminals, test both sets.

**Test a three-slot receptacle for grounding.** With the power on, place one probe of the tester in the short (hot) slot, and the other in the U shaped grounding hole. The tester should glow. If it does not glow, place a probe in the long (neutral) slot and one in the grounding hole. If the tester glows, the hot and neutral wires are reversed. If tester does not glow in either position, the receptacle is not grounded.

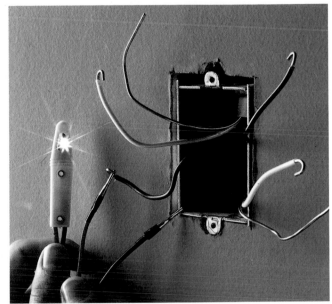

**Test for hot wires.** Occasionally, you may need to determine which wire is hot. With the power turned off, carefully separate all ends of wires so that they do not touch each other or anything else. Restore power to the circuit at the main service panel. Touch one probe of the neon tester to the bare grounding wire or grounded metal box, and the other probe to the ends of each of the wires. Check all wires. If the tester glows, the wire is hot. Label the hot wire for identification, and turn off power at the service panel before continuing work.

## How to Test a Two-slot Receptacle for Grounding

**1** With the power turned on, place one probe of the neon tester in each slot. The tester should glow. If it does not glow, then there is no power to the receptacle.

**2** Place one probe of the tester in the short (hot) slot, and touch the other probe to the coverplate screw. The screw head must be free of paint, dirt, and grease. If the tester glows, the receptacle box is grounded. If it does not glow, proceed to step 3.

**3** Place one probe of the tester in the long (neutral) slot, and touch the other to the coverplate screw. If the tester glows, the receptacle box is grounded but hot and neutral wires are reversed. If tester does not glow, the box is not grounded.

# Repairing & Replacing Receptacles

Receptacles are easy to repair. After shutting off power to the receptacle circuit, remove the coverplate and inspect the receptacle for any obvious problems such as a loose or broken connection, or wire ends that are dirty or oxidized. Remember that a problem at one receptacle may affect other receptacles in the same circuit. If the cause of a faulty receptacle is not readily apparent, test other receptacles in the circuit for power (page 120).

When replacing a receptacle, check the amperage rating of the circuit at the main service panel, and buy a replacement receptacle with the correct amperage rating.

When installing a new receptacle, always test for grounding (pages 120 to 121). Never install a three-slot receptacle where no grounding exists. Instead, install a two-slot polarized, or GFCI receptacle.

### Everything You Need:

Tools: neon circuit tester, screwdriver, vacuum cleaner (if needed).

Materials: fine sandpaper, anti-oxidant paste (if needed).

## How to Repair a Receptacle

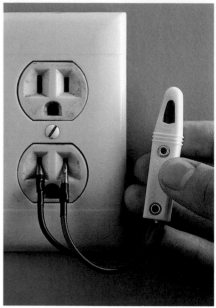

**1** Turn off power at the main service panel. Test the receptacle for power with a neon circuit tester (page 120). Test both ends of a duplex receptacle. Remove the coverplate, using a screwdriver.

**2** Remove the mounting screws that hold the receptacle to the box. Carefully pull the receptacle from the box. Take care not to touch any bare wires.

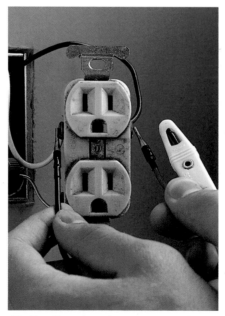

**3** Confirm that the power to the receptacle is off (page 120), using a neon circuit tester. If wires are attached to both sets of screw terminals, test both sets. The tester should not glow. If it does, you must turn off the correct circuit at the service panel.

**4** If the ends of the wires appear darkened or dirty, disconnect them one at a time, and clean them with fine sandpaper. If the wires are aluminum, apply an anti-oxidant paste before reconnecting. Anti-oxidant paste is available at hardware stores.

**5** Tighten all connections, using a screwdriver. Take care not to overtighten and strip the screws.

**6** Check the box for dirt or dust and, if necessary, clean it with a vacuum cleaner and narrow nozzle attachment.

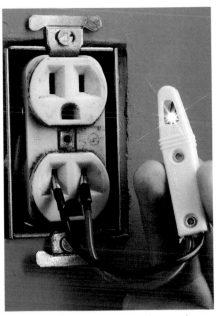

**7** Reinstall the receptacle, and turn on power at the main service panel. Test the receptacle for power with a neon circuit tester. If the receptacle does not work, check other receptacles in the circuit before making a replacement.

## How to Replace a Receptacle

**1** To replace a receptacle, repeat steps 1 to 3 on the opposite page. With the power off, label each wire for its location on the receptacle screw terminals, using masking tape and a felt-tipped pen.

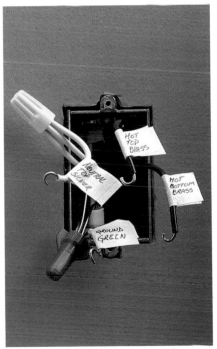

**2** Disconnect all wires and remove the receptacle.

**3** Replace the receptacle with one rated for the correct amperage and voltage (page 94). Replace coverplate, and turn on power. Test receptacle with a neon circuit tester (pages 120 to 121).

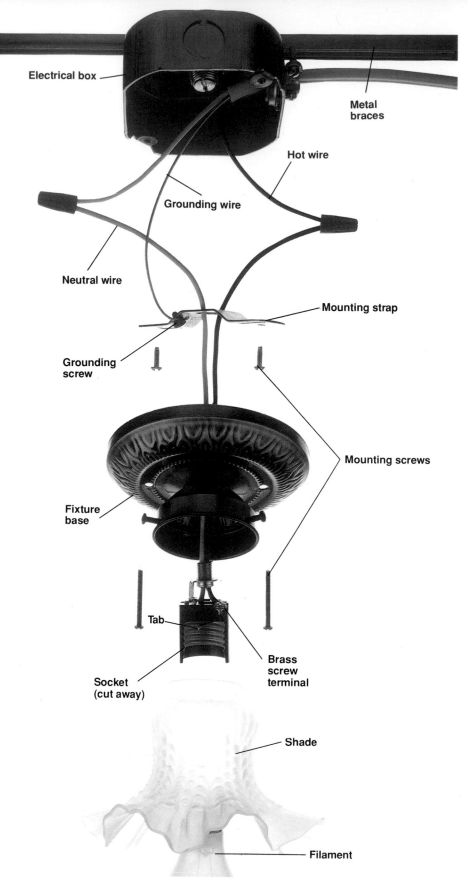

Electrical box

Metal braces

Hot wire

Grounding wire

Neutral wire

Mounting strap

Grounding screw

Mounting screws

Fixture base

Tab

Brass screw terminal

Socket (cut away)

Shade

Filament

**In a typical incandescent light fixture**, a black hot wire is connected to a brass screw terminal on the socket. Power flows to a small tab at the bottom of the metal socket and through a metal filament inside the bulb. The power heats the filament and causes it to glow. The current then flows through the threaded portion of the socket and through the white neutral wire back to the main service panel.

# Repairing & Replacing Incandescent Light Fixtures

Incandescent light fixtures are attached permanently to ceilings or walls. They include wall-hung sconces, ceiling-hung globe fixtures, recessed light fixtures, and chandeliers. Most incandescent light fixtures are easy to repair, using basic tools and inexpensive parts.

Track lights, another type of incandescent light fixture, are difficult to fix and should be repaired or replaced by an electrician.

If a light fixture fails, always make sure the light bulb is screwed in tightly and is not burned out. A faulty light bulb is the most common cause of light fixture failure. If the light fixture is controlled by a wall switch, also check the switch as a possible source of problems (pages 108 to 109).

Light fixtures can fail because the sockets or built-in switches wear out. Some fixtures have sockets and switches that can be removed for minor repairs. These parts are held to the base of the fixture with mounting screws or clips. Other fixtures have sockets and switches that are joined permanently to the base. If this type of fixture fails, purchase and install a new light fixture.

Damage to light fixtures often occurs because homeowners install light bulbs with wattage ratings that are too high. Prevent overheating and light fixture failures by using only light

124

bulbs that match the wattage ratings printed on the fixtures.

Techniques for repairing fluorescent lights are different from those for incandescent lights. Refer to pages 134 to 139 to repair or replace a fluorescent light fixture.

## Everything You Need:

Tools: neon circuit tester, screwdrivers, continuity tester, combination tool.

Materials: replacement parts, as needed.

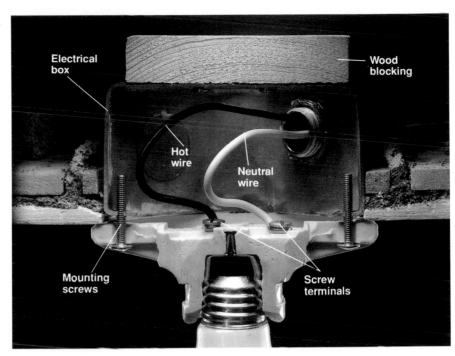

**Before 1959,** incandescent light fixtures (shown cut away) often were mounted directly to an electrical box or to plaster lath. Electrical codes now require that fixtures be attached to mounting straps that are anchored to the electrical boxes (page opposite). If you have a light fixture attached to plaster lath, install an approved electrical box with a mounting strap to support the fixture (pages 104 to 107).

| Problem | Repair |
|---|---|
| Wall- or ceiling-mounted fixture flickers, or does not light. | 1. Check for faulty light bulb.<br>2. Check wall switch, and repair or replace, if needed (pages 108 to 117).<br>3. Check for loose wire connections in electrical box.<br>4. Test socket, and replace if needed (pages 126 to 127).<br>5. Replace light fixture (page 128). |
| Built-in switch on fixture does not work. | 1. Check for faulty light bulb.<br>2. Check for loose wire connections on switch.<br>3. Replace switch (page 127).<br>4. Replace light fixture (page 128). |
| Chandelier flickers or does not light. | 1. Check for faulty light bulb.<br>2. Check wall switch, and repair or replace, if needed (pages 108 to 117).<br>3. Check for loose wire connections in electrical box.<br>4. Test sockets and fixture wires, and replace if needed (pages 132 to 133). |
| Recessed fixture flickers or does not light. | 1. Check for faulty light bulb.<br>2. Check wall switch, and repair or replace, if needed (pages 108 to 117).<br>3. Check for loose wire connections in electrical box.<br>4. Test fixture, and replace if needed (pages 129 to 131). |

## How to Remove a Light Fixture & Test a Socket

**1** Turn off the power to the light fixture at the main service panel. Remove the light bulb and any shade or globe, then remove the mounting screws holding the fixture base to the electrical box or mounting strap. Carefully pull the fixture base away from box.

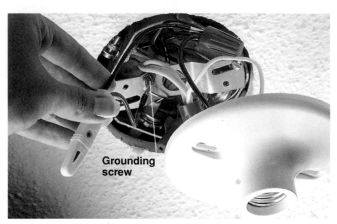

**2** Test for power by touching one probe of a neon circuit tester to green grounding screw, then inserting other probe into each wire nut. Tester should not glow. If it does, there is still power entering box. Return to the service panel and turn off power to correct circuit.

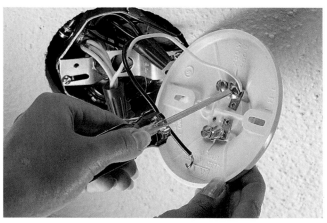

**3** Disconnect the light fixture base by loosening the screw terminals. If fixture has wire leads instead of screw terminals, remove the light fixture base by unscrewing the wire nuts.

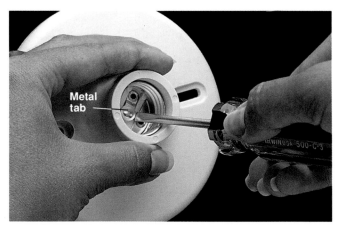

**4** Adjust the metal tab at the bottom of the fixture socket by prying it up slightly with a small screwdriver. This adjustment will improve the contact between the socket and the light bulb.

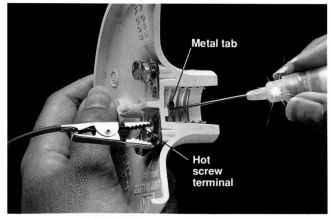

**5** Test the socket (shown cut away) by attaching the clip of a continuity tester to the hot screw terminal (or black wire lead), and touching probe of tester to metal tab in bottom of socket. Tester should glow. If not, socket is faulty and must be replaced.

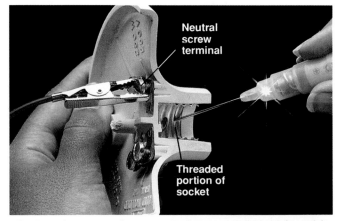

**6** Attach tester clip to neutral screw terminal (or white wire lead), and touch probe to threaded portion of socket. Tester should glow. If not, socket is faulty and must be replaced. If socket is permanently attached, replace the fixture (page 128).

## How to Replace a Socket

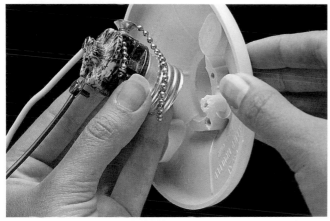

**1** Remove light fixture (steps 1 to 3, page opposite). Remove the socket from the fixture. Socket may be held by a screw, clip, or retaining ring. Disconnect wires attached to the socket.

**2** Purchase an identical replacement socket. Connect white wire to silver screw terminal on socket, and connect black wire to brass screw terminal. Attach socket to fixture base, and reinstall fixture.

## How to Test & Replace a Built-in Light Switch

Retaining ring

Switch leads

**1** Remove light fixture (steps 1 to 3, page opposite). Unscrew the retaining ring holding the switch.

**2** Label the wires connected to the switch leads. Disconnect the switch leads and remove switch.

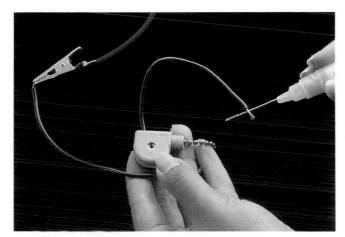

**3** Test switch by attaching clip of continuity tester to one of the switch leads, and holding tester probe to the other lead. Operate switch control. If switch is good, tester will glow when switch is in one position, but not both.

**4** If the switch is faulty, purchase and install an exact duplicate switch. Remount the light fixture, and turn on the power at the main service panel.

# How to Replace an Incandescent Light Fixture

**1** Turn off the power and remove the old light fixture, following the directions for standard light fixtures (page 126, steps 1 to 3) or chandeliers (pages 132 to 133, steps 1 to 4).

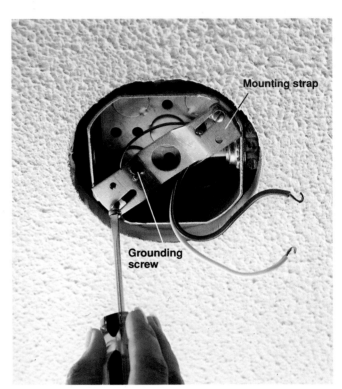

**2** Attach a mounting strap to the electrical box, if box does not already have one. The mounting strap, included with the new light fixture, has a preinstalled grounding screw.

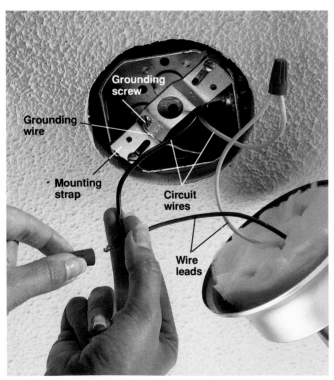

**3** Connect the circuit wires to the base of new fixture, using wire nuts. Connect the white wire lead to the white circuit wire, and the black wire lead to the black circuit wire. Pigtail the bare copper grounding wire to the grounding screw on the mounting strap.

**4** Attach the light fixture base to the mounting strap, using the mounting screws. Attach the globe, and install a light bulb with a wattage rating that is the same or lower than the rating indicated on the fixture. Turn on the power at the main service panel.

## Repairing & Replacing Recessed Light Fixtures

Most problems with recessed light fixtures occur because heat builds up inside the metal canister and melts the insulation on the socket wires. On some recessed light fixtures, sockets with damaged wires can be removed and replaced. However, most newer fixtures have sockets that cannot be removed. With this type, you will need to buy a new fixture if the socket wires are damaged.

When buying a new recessed light fixture, choose a replacement that matches the old fixture. Install the new fixture in the metal mounting frame that is already in place.

Make sure building insulation is at least 3" away from the metal canister on a recessed light fixture. Insulation that fits too closely traps heat and can damage the socket wires.

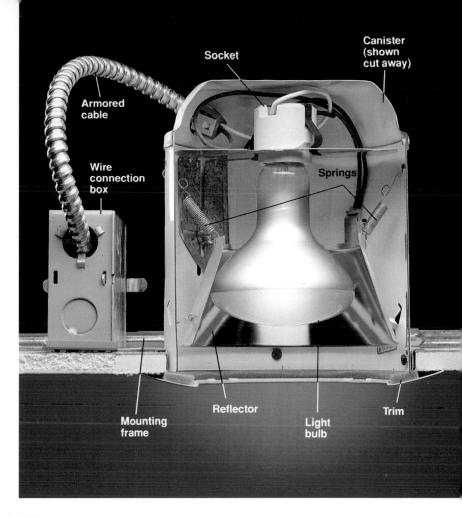

Armored cable

Wire connection box

Socket

Canister (shown cut away)

Springs

Reflector

Mounting frame

Light bulb

Trim

### How to Remove & Test a Recessed Light Fixture

Spring

Reflector

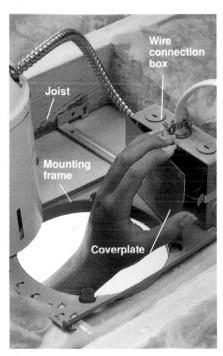

Wire connection box

Joist

Mounting frame

Coverplate

**1** Turn off the power to the light fixture at the main service panel. Remove the trim, light bulb, and reflector. The reflector is held to the canister with small springs or mounting clips.

**2** Loosen the screws or clips holding the canister to the mounting frame. Carefully raise the canister and set it away from the frame opening.

**3** Remove the coverplate on the wire connection box. The box is attached to the mounting frame between the ceiling joists.

(continued next page)

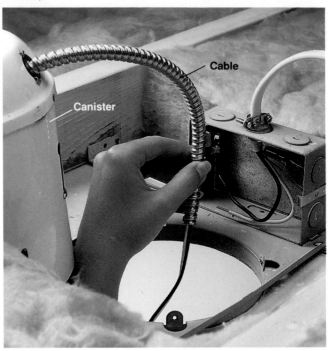

**4** Test for power by touching one probe of neon circuit tester to grounded wire connection box, and inserting other probe into each wire nut. Tester should not glow. If it does, there is still power entering box. Return to the service panel and turn off correct circuit.

**5** Disconnect the white and black circuit wires by removing the wire nuts. Pull the armored cable from the wire connection box. Remove the canister through the frame opening.

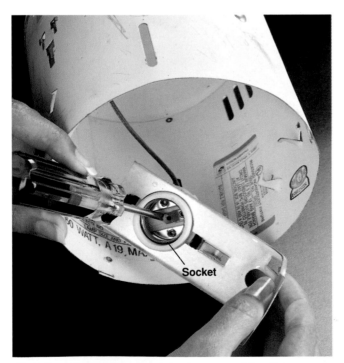

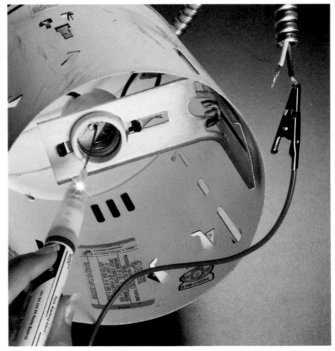

**6** Adjust the metal tab at the bottom of the fixture socket by prying it up slightly with a small screwdriver. This adjustment will improve contact with the light bulb.

**7** Test the socket by attaching the clip of a continuity tester to the black fixture wire and touching tester probe to the metal tab in bottom of the socket. Attach the tester clip to white fixture wire, and touch probe to the threaded metal socket. Tester should glow for both tests. If not, then socket is faulty. Replace the socket (page 127), or install a new light fixture (page opposite).

# How to Replace a Recessed Light Fixture

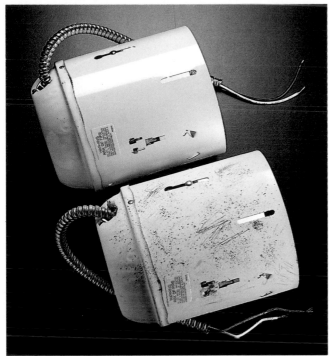

**1** Remove the old light fixture (pages 129 to 130). Buy a new fixture that matches the old fixture. Although new light fixture comes with its own mounting frame, it is easier to mount the new fixture using the frame that is already in place.

**2** Set the fixture canister inside the ceiling cavity, and thread the fixture wires through the opening in the wire connection box. Push the armored cable into the wire connection box to secure it.

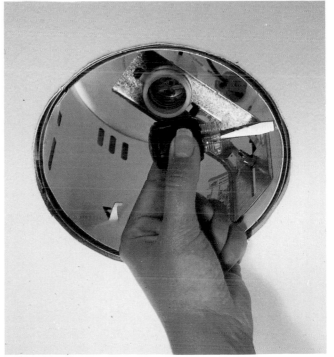

**3** Connect the white fixture wire to the white circuit wire, and the black fixture wire to the black circuit wire, using wire nuts. Attach the coverplate to the wire connection box. Make sure any building insulation is at least 3" from canister and wire connection box.

**4** Position the canister inside the mounting frame, and attach the mounting screws or clips. Attach the reflector and trim. Install a light bulb with a wattage rating that is the same or lower than rating indicated on the fixture. Turn on power at main service panel.

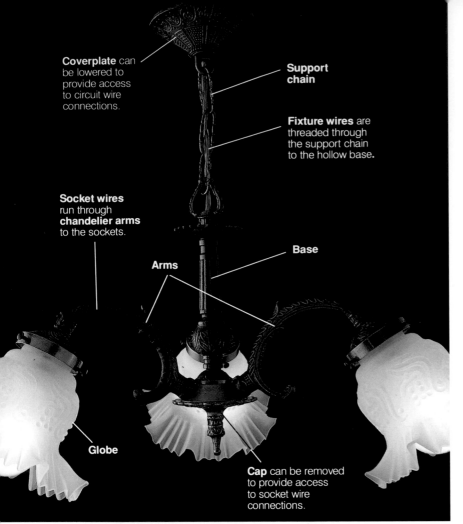

**Coverplate** can be lowered to provide access to circuit wire connections.

**Support chain**

**Fixture wires** are threaded through the support chain to the hollow base.

**Socket wires** run through **chandelier arms** to the sockets.

**Arms**

**Base**

**Globe**

**Cap** can be removed to provide access to socket wire connections.

# Repairing Chandeliers

Repairing a chandelier requires special care. Because chandeliers are heavy, it is a good idea to work with a helper when removing a chandelier. Support the fixture to prevent its weight from pulling against the wires.

Chandeliers have two fixture wires that are threaded through the support chain from the electrical box to the hollow base of the chandelier. The socket wires connect to the fixture wires inside this base.

Fixture wires are identified as hot and neutral. Look closely for printed lettering or a colored stripe on one of the wires. This is the neutral wire that is connected to the white circuit wire and white socket wire. The other, unmarked, fixture wire is hot, and is connected to the black wires.

If you have a new chandelier, it may have a grounding wire that runs through the support chain to the electrical box. If this wire is present, make sure it is connected to the grounding wires in the electrical box.

## How to Repair a Chandelier

**1** Label any lights that are not working, using masking tape. Turn off power to the fixture at the main service panel. Remove light bulbs and all shades or globes.

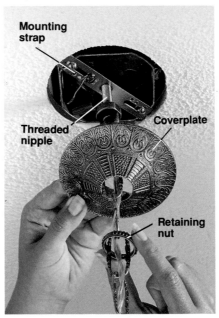

**Mounting strap**

**Threaded nipple**

**Coverplate**

**Retaining nut**

**2** Unscrew the retaining nut and lower the decorative coverplate away from the electrical box. Most chandeliers are supported by a threaded nipple attached to a mounting strap.

**Mounting strap**

**Mounting bolt**

**Bolt cap nut**

**Mounting variation:** Some chandeliers are supported only by the coverplate that is bolted to the electrical box mounting strap. These types do not have a threaded nipple.

132

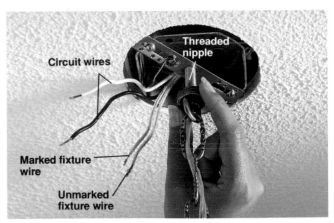

**3** Test for power by touching one probe of neon circuit tester to the green grounding screw, and inserting other probe into each wire nut. Tester should not glow. If it does, there is still power entering box. Return to service panel and turn off power to correct circuit.

**4** Disconnect fixture wires by removing the wire nuts. Marked fixture wire is neutral, and is connected to white circuit wire. Unmarked fixture wire is hot, and is connected to black circuit wire. Unscrew threaded nipple and carefully place chandelier on a flat surface.

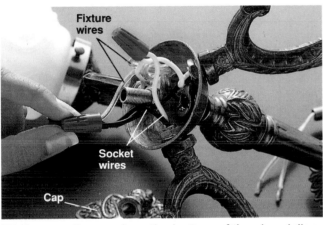

**5** Remove the cap from the bottom of the chandelier, exposing the wire connections inside the hollow base. Disconnect the black socket wires from the unmarked fixture wire, and disconnect the white socket wires from the marked fixture wire.

**6** Test socket by attaching clip of continuity tester to black socket wire, and touching probe to tab in socket. Repeat test with threaded portion of socket and white socket wire. Tester should glow for both tests. If not, the socket is faulty and must be replaced.

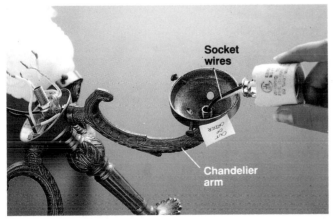

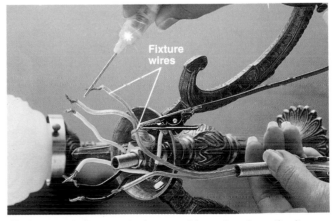

**7** Remove a faulty socket by loosening any mounting screws or clips, and pulling the socket and socket wires out of the fixture arm. Purchase and install a new chandelier socket, threading the socket wires through the fixture arm.

**8** Test each fixture wire by attaching clip of continuity tester to one end of wire, and touching probe to other end. If tester does not glow, wire is faulty and must be replaced. Install new wires, if needed, then reassemble and rehang the chandelier.

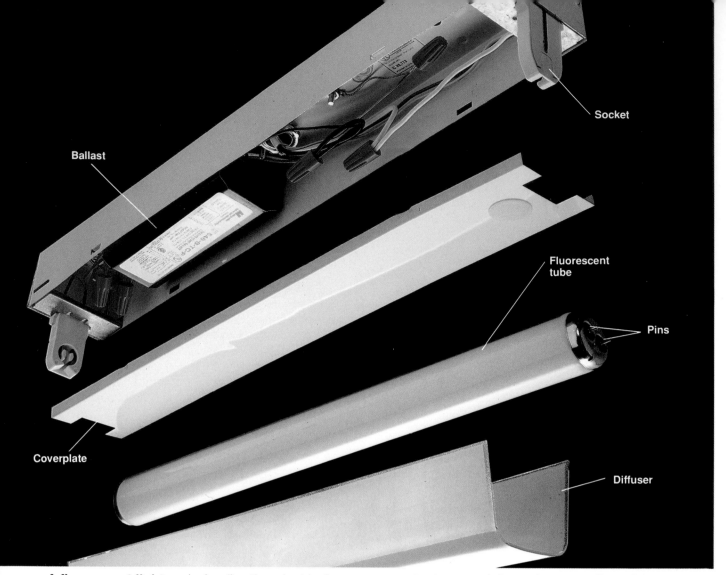

**A fluorescent light** works by directing electrical current through a special gas-filled **tube** that glows when energized. A white transluscent **diffuser** protects the fluorescent tube and softens the light. A **coverplate** protects a special transformer, called a **ballast**. The ballast regulates the flow of 120-volt household current to the **sockets**. The sockets transfer power to metal **pins** that extend into the tube.

Image labels: Ballast, Socket, Fluorescent tube, Pins, Coverplate, Diffuser

# Repairing & Replacing Fluorescent Lights

Fluorescent lights are relatively trouble-free, and use less energy than incandescent lights. A typical fluorescent tube lasts about three years, and produces two to four times as much light per watt as a standard incandescent light bulb.

The most frequent problem with a fluorescent light fixture is a worn-out tube. If a fluorescent light fixture begins to flicker, or does not light fully, remove and examine the tube. If the tube has bent or broken pins, or black discoloration near the ends, replace it. Light gray discoloration is normal in working fluorescent tubes. When replacing an old tube, read the wattage rating printed on the glass surface, and buy a new tube with a matching rating.

Never dispose of old tubes by breaking them. Fluorescent tubes contain a small amount of hazardous mercury. Check with your local environmental control agency or health department for disposal guidelines.

Fluorescent light fixtures also can malfunction if the sockets are cracked or worn. Inexpensive replacement sockets are available at any hardware store, and can be installed in a few minutes.

If a fixture does not work even after the tube and sockets have been serviced, the ballast probably is defective. Faulty ballasts may leak a black, oily substance, and can cause a fluorescent light

| Problem | Repair |
|---|---|
| Tube flickers, or lights partially. | 1. Rotate tube to make sure it is seated properly in the sockets.<br>2. Replace tube (page 136) and the starter (where present) if tube is discolored or if pins are bent or broken.<br>3. Replace the ballast (page 138) if replacement cost is reasonable. Otherwise, replace the entire fixture (page 139). |
| Tube does not light. | 1. Check wall switch, and repair or replace, if needed (pages 108 to 117).<br>2. Rotate the tube to make sure it is seated properly in the sockets.<br>3. Replace tube (page 136) and the starter (where present) if tube is discolored or if pins are bent or broken.<br>4. Replace sockets if they are chipped, or if tube does not seat properly (page 137).<br>5. Replace the ballast (page 138) or the entire fixture (page 139). |
| Noticeable black substance around ballast. | Replace ballast (page 138) If replacement cost is reasonable. Otherwise, replace the entire fixture (page 139). |
| Fixture hums. | Replace ballast (page 138) If replacement cost is reasonable. Otherwise, replace the entire fixture (page 139). |

fixture to make a loud humming sound. Although ballasts can be replaced, always check prices before buying a new ballast. It may be cheaper to purchase and install a new fluorescent fixture rather than to replace the ballast in an old fluorescent light fixture.

**Everything You Need:**

Tools: screwdriver, ratchet wrench, combination tool, neon circuit tester.

Materials: replacement tubes, starters, or ballast (if needed); replacement fluorescent light fixture (if needed).

**Older fluorescent lights** may have a small cylindrical device, called a starter, located near one of the sockets. When a tube begins to flicker, replace both the tube and the starter. Turn off the power, then remove the starter by pushing it slightly and turning counterclockwise. Install a replacement that matches the old starter.

## How to Replace a Fluorescent Tube

**1** Turn off power to the light fixture at the main service panel. Remove the diffuser to expose the fluorescent tube.

**2** Remove the fluorescent tube by rotating it ¼ turn in either direction and sliding the tube out of the sockets. Inspect the pins at the end of the tube. Tubes with bent or broken pins should be replaced.

**3** Inspect the ends of the fluorescent tube for discoloration. New tube in good working order (top) shows no discoloration. Normal, working tube (middle) may have gray color. A worn-out tube (bottom) shows black discoloration.

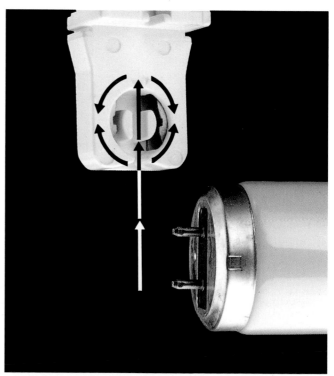

**4** Install a new tube with the same wattage rating as the old tube. Insert the tube so that pins slide fully into sockets, then twist tube ¼ turn in either direction until it is locked securely. Reattach the diffuser, and turn on the power at the main service panel.

# How to Replace a Socket

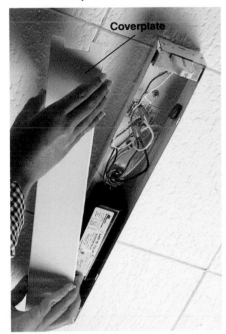

**Coverplate**

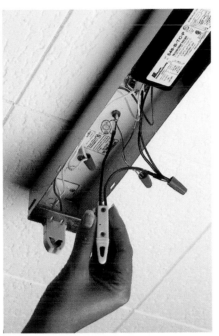

**1** Turn off the power at the main service panel. Remove the diffuser, fluorescent tube, and the coverplate.

**2** Test for power by touching one probe of a neon circuit tester to the grounding screw, and inserting the other probe into each wire nut. Tester should not glow. If it does, power is still entering the box. Return to the service panel and turn off correct circuit.

**3** Remove the faulty socket from the fixture housing. Some sockets slide out, while others must be unscrewed.

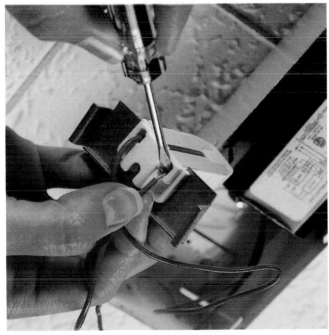

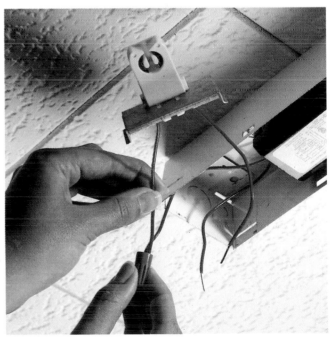

**4** Disconnect wires attached to socket. For push-in fittings (above) remove the wires by inserting a small screwdriver into the release openings. Some sockets have screw terminal connections, while others have preattached wires that must be cut before the socket can be removed.

**5** Purchase and install a new socket. If socket has preattached wire leads, connect the leads to the ballast wires using wire nuts. Replace coverplate and diffuser, then turn on power at the main service panel.

## How to Replace a Ballast

**1** Turn off the power at the main service panel, then remove the diffuser, fluorescent tube, and coverplate. Test for power, using a neon circuit tester (step 2, page 137).

**2** Remove the sockets from the fixture housing by sliding them out, or by removing the mounting screws and lifting the sockets out.

**3** Disconnect the wires attached to the sockets by pushing a small screwdriver into the release openings (above), by loosening the screw terminals, or by cutting wires to within 2" of sockets.

**4** Remove the old ballast, using a ratchet wrench or screwdriver. Make sure to support the ballast so it does not fall.

**5** Install a new ballast that has the same ratings as the old ballast.

**6** Attach the ballast wires to the socket wires, using wire nuts, screw terminal connections, or push-in fittings. Reinstall the coverplate, fluorescent tube, and diffuser. Turn on power to the light fixture at the main service panel.

# How to Replace a Fluorescent Light Fixture

**1** Turn off power to the light fixture at the main service panel. Remove diffuser, tube, and coverplate. Test for power, using a neon circuit tester (step 2, page 137).

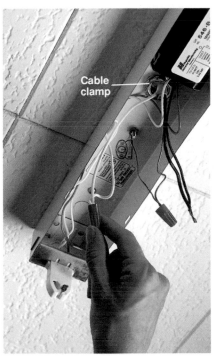

**2** Disconnect the insulated circuit wires and the bare copper grounding wire from the light fixture. Loosen the cable clamp holding the circuit wires.

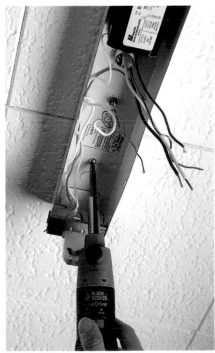

**3** Unbolt the fixture from the wall or ceiling, and carefully remove it. Make sure to support the fixture so it does not fall.

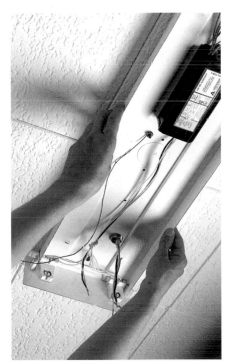

**4** Position the new fixture, threading the circuit wires through the knockout opening in the back of the fixture. Bolt the fixture in place so it is firmly anchored to framing members.

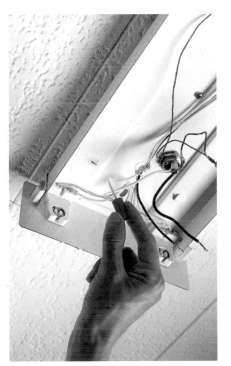

**5** Connect the circuit wires to the fixture wires, using wire nuts. Follow the wiring diagram included with the new fixture. Tighten the cable clamp holding the circuit wires.

**6** Attach the fixture coverplate, then install the fluorescent tubes, and attach the diffuser. Turn on power to the fixture at the main service panel.

# Replacing a Lamp Socket

Next to the cord plug, the most common source of trouble in a lamp is a worn light bulb socket. When a lamp socket assembly fails, the problem is usually with the socket-switch unit, although replacement sockets may include other parts you do not need.

Lamp failure is not always caused by a bad socket. You can avoid unnecessary repairs by checking the lamp cord, plug and light bulb before replacing the socket.

**Before You Start:**

Tools & Materials: replacement socket, continuity tester, screwdriver.

Tip: When replacing a lamp socket, you can improve a standard ON-OFF lamp by installing a three-way socket.

## Types of Sockets

**Socket-mounted switch** types are usually interchangeable: choose a replacement you prefer. Clockwise from top left: twist knob, remote switch, pull chain, push lever.

# How to Repair or Replace a Lamp Socket

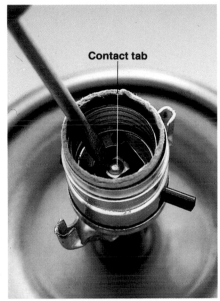

**1** Unplug lamp. Remove shade, light bulb and harp (shade bracket). Scrape contact tab clean with a small screwdriver, Pry contact tab up slightly if flattened inside socket. Replace bulb, plug in lamp and test. If lamp does not work, unplug, remove bulb and continue with next step.

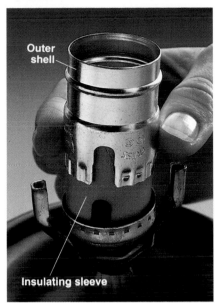

**2** Squeeze outer shell of socket near PRESS marking, and lift it off. On older lamps, socket may be held by screws found at the base of the screw socket. Slip off cardboard insulating sleeve. If sleeve is damaged, replace entire socket.

**3** Check for loose wire connections on screw terminals. Refasten any loose connections, then reassemble lamp and test. If connections are not loose, remove the wires, lift out the socket and continue with the next step.

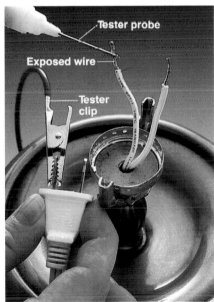

**4** Test for lamp cord problems with continuity tester. Place clip of tester on one prong of plug. Touch probe to one exposed wire, then to the other wire. Repeat test with other prong of plug. If tester fails to light for either prong, then replace the cord and plug. Retest the lamp.

**5** If cord and plug are functional, then choose a replacement socket marked with the same amp and volt ratings as the old socket. One half of flat-cord lamp wire is covered by insulation that is ridged or marked: attach this wire to the silver screw terminal. Connect other wire to brass screw.

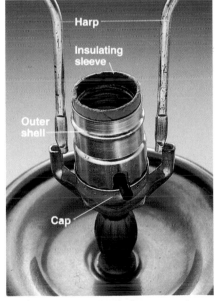

**6** Slide insulating sleeve and outer shell over socket so that socket and screw terminals are fully covered and switch fits into sleeve slot. Press socket assembly down into cap until socket locks into place. Replace harp, light bulb and shade.

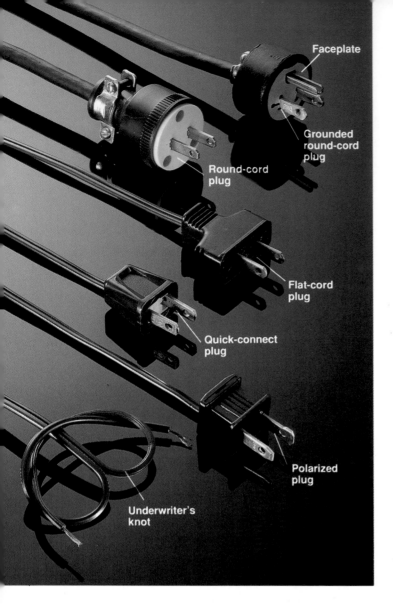

Faceplate

Grounded round-cord plug

Round-cord plug

Flat-cord plug

Quick-connect plug

Polarized plug

Underwriter's knot

# Replacing a Plug

Replace an electrical plug whenever you notice bent or loose prongs, a cracked or damaged casing, or a missing insulating faceplate. A damaged plug poses a shock and fire hazard.

Replacement plugs are available in different styles to match common appliance cords. Always choose a replacement that is similar to the original plug. Flat-cord and quick-connect plugs are used with light-duty appliances, like lamps and radios. Round-cord plugs are used with larger appliances, including those that have three-prong grounding plugs.

Some appliances use polarized plugs. A polarized plug has one wide prong and one narrow prong, corresponding to the hot and neutral slots found in a standard receptacle. Polarization (page 82) ensures that the cord wires are aligned correctly with the receptacle slots.

If there is room in the plug body, tie the individual wires in an underwriter's knot to secure the plug to the cord.

**Everything You Need:**

Tools: combination tool, needlenose pliers, screwdriver.

Materials: replacement plug.

## How to Install a Quick-connect Plug

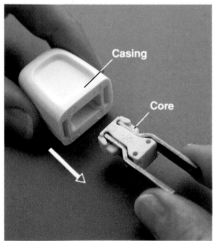

Casing

Core

**1** Squeeze the prongs of the new quick-connect plug together slightly and pull the plug core from the casing. Cut the old plug from the flat-cord wire with a combination tool, leaving a clean-cut end.

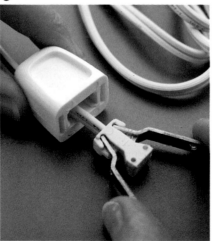

**2** Feed unstripped wire through rear of plug casing. Spread prongs, then insert wire into opening in rear of core. Squeeze prongs together; spikes inside core penetrate cord. Slide casing over core until it snaps into place.

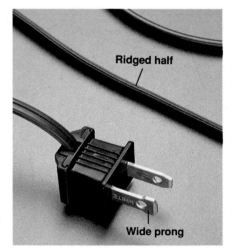

Ridged half

Wide prong

**When replacing a polarized plug,** make sure that the ridged half of the cord lines up with the wider (neutral) prong of the plug.

## How to Replace a Round-cord Plug

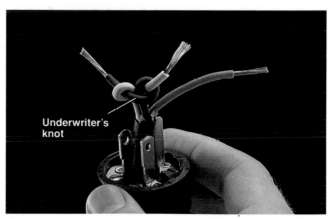

**1** Cut off round cord near the old plug, using a combination tool. Remove the insulating faceplate on the new plug, and feed cord through rear of plug. Strip about 3" of outer insulation from the round cord. Strip ¾" insulation from the individual wires.

**2** Tie an underwriter's knot with the black and white wires. Make sure the knot is located close to the edge of the stripped outer insulation. Pull the cord so that the knot slides into the plug body.

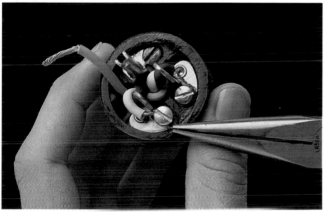

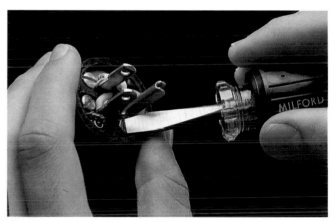

**3** Hook end of black wire clockwise around brass screw, and white wire around silver screw. On a three-prong plug, attach third wire to grounding screw. If necessary, excess grounding wire can be cut away.

**4** Tighten the screws securely, making sure the copper wires do not touch each other. Replace the insulating faceplate.

## How to Replace a Flat-cord Plug

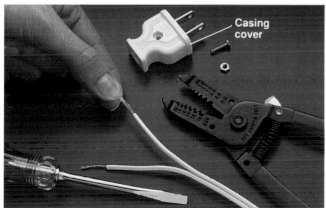

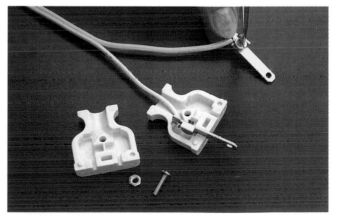

**1** Cut old plug from cord using a combination tool. Pull apart the two halves of the flat cord so that about 2" of wire are separated. Strip ¾" insulation from each half. Remove casing cover on new plug.

**2** Hook ends of wires clockwise around the screw terminals, and tighten the screw terminals securely. Reassemble the plug casing. Some plugs may have an insulating faceplate that must be installed.

**Home doorbell system** is powered by a transformer that reduces 120-volt current to low-voltage current of 20 volts or less. Current flows from the transformer to one or more push-button switches. When pushed, the switch activates a magnetic coil inside the chime unit, causing a plunger to strike a musical tuning bar.

# Fixing & Replacing Doorbells

Most doorbell problems are caused by loose wire connections or worn-out switches. Reconnecting loose wires or replacing a switch requires only a few minutes. Doorbell problems also can occur if the chime unit becomes dirty or worn, or if the low-voltage transformer burns out. Both parts are easy to replace. Because doorbells operate at low voltage, the switches and the chime unit can be serviced without turning off power to the system. However, when replacing a transformer, always turn off the power at the main service panel.

Most houses have other low-voltage transformers in addition to the doorbell transformer. These transformers control heating and air-conditioning thermostats (pages 150 to 157), or other low-voltage systems. When testing and repairing a doorbell system, it is important to identify the correct transformer. A doorbell transformer has a voltage rating of 20 volts or less. This rating is printed on the face of the transformer. A doorbell transformer often is located near the main service panel, and in some homes is attached directly to the service panel.

The transformer that controls a heating/air-conditioning thermostat system is located near the furnace, and has a voltage rating of 24 volts or more.

Occasionally, a doorbell problem is caused by a broken low-voltage wire somewhere in the system. You can test for wire breaks with a battery-operated multi-tester. If the test indicates a break, new low-voltage wires must be installed between the transformer and the switches, or between the switches and chime unit. Replacing low-voltage wires is not a difficult job, but it can be time-consuming. You may choose to have an electrician do this work.

**Everything You Need:**

Tools: continuity tester, screwdriver, multi-tester, needlenose pliers.

Materials: cotton swab, rubbing alcohol, replacement doorbell switch (if needed), masking tape, replacement chime unit (if needed).

144

# How to Test a Doorbell System

**1** Remove the mounting screws holding the doorbell switch to the house.

**2** Carefully pull the switch away from the wall.

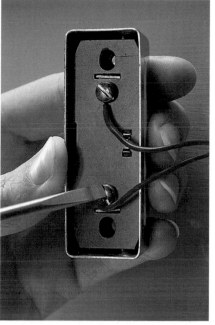

**3** Check wire connections on the switch. If wires are loose, reconnect them to the screw terminals. Test the doorbell by pressing the button. If the doorbell still does not work, disconnect the switch and test it with a continuity tester.

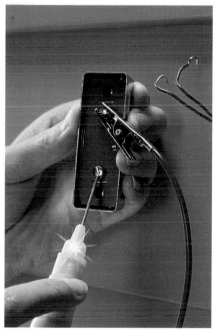

**4** Test the switch by attaching the clip of a continuity tester to one screw terminal, and touching the probe to the other screw terminal. Press the switch button. Tester should glow. If not, then the switch is faulty and must be replaced (page 148).

**5** Twist the doorbell switch wires together temporarily to test the other parts of the doorbell system.

Transformer

**6** Locate the doorbell transformer, often located near the main service panel. Transformer may be attached to an electrical box, or may be attached directly to the side of the service panel.

(continued next page)

**7** Identify the doorbell transformer by reading its voltage rating. Doorbell transformers have a voltage rating of 20 volts or less.

**8** Turn off power to transformer at main service panel. Remove cover on electrical box, and test wires for power (step 3, page 155). Reconnect any loose wires. Replace taped connections with wire nut connections. Reattach coverplate.

**9** Inspect the low-voltage wire connections, and reconnect any loose wires, using needlenose pliers. Turn on power to the transformer at the main service panel.

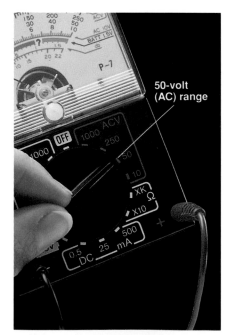

**10** Set the dial of multi-tester to the 50-volt (AC) range.

**11** Touch the probes of the multi-tester to the low-voltage screw terminals on the transformer.

**12** If transformer is operating properly, multi-tester will detect power that is within 2 volts of transformer's rating. If not, then transformer is faulty and must be replaced (page 155).

**13** Remove the coverplate on the doorbell chime unit.

**14** Inspect the low-voltage wire connections, and reconnect any loose wires.

**15** Test to make sure chime unit is receiving proper current with a multi-tester set to 50-volt (AC) range. Touch probes of tester to screw terminals marked TRANS-FORMER (or TRANS) and FRONT.

**16** If the multi-tester detects power within 2 volts of the transformer rating, then the chime unit is receiving proper current. If multi-tester detects no power, or very low power, then there is a break in the low-voltage wiring, and new wires must be installed.

**17** If necessary, repeat test for rear doorbell wires. Hold probes to terminals marked TRANS-FORMER (or TRANS) and REAR. Multi-tester should detect power within 2 volts of transformer's rating. If not, there is a break in wiring, and new wires must be installed.

**18** Clean the chime plungers with a cotton swab dipped in rubbing alcohol. Reassemble door-bell switches, then test the system by pushing one of the switches. If doorbell still does not work, then the chime unit is faulty and must be replaced (page 148).

## How to Replace a Doorbell Switch

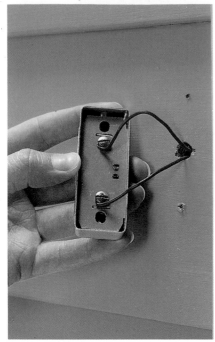

**1** Remove the doorbell switch mounting screws, and carefully pull the switch away from the wall.

**2** Disconnect wires from switch. Tape wires to the wall to prevent them from slipping into the wall cavity. Purchase a new doorbell switch, and connect wires to screw terminals on new switch. (Wires are interchangeable, and can be connected to either screw terminal.)

**3** Anchor the switch to the wall with the mounting screws.

## How to Replace a Doorbell Chime Unit

**1** Turn off power to the doorbell system at the main service panel. Remove the coverplate from the old chime unit.

**2** Using masking tape, label the low-voltage wires FRONT, REAR, or TRANS to identify their screw terminal locations. Disconnect the low-voltage wires.

**3** Unscrew the mounting screws, and remove the old chime unit.

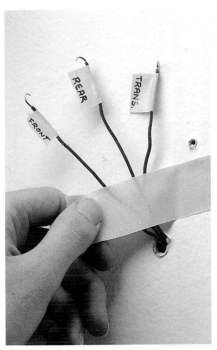

**4** Tape the wires to the wall to prevent them from slipping into the wall cavity.

**5** Purchase a new chime unit that matches the voltage rating of the old unit. Thread the low-voltage wires through the base of the new chime unit.

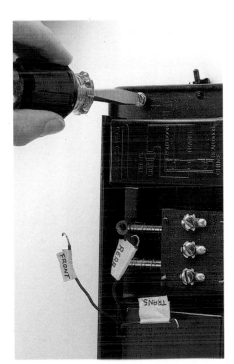

**6** Attach the chime unit to the wall, using the mounting screws included with the installation kit.

**7** Connect the low-voltage wires to the screw terminals on the new chime unit.

**8** Attach the coverplate and turn on the power at the main service panel.

**Electronic programmable thermostats** can be set to make up to four temperature changes each day. They are available in low-voltage designs (right) for central heating/cooling systems, and in line-voltage designs (left) for electric baseboard heating. Most electronic programmable thermostats have an internal battery that saves the program in case of a power failure.

# Fixing & Replacing Thermostats

A thermostat is a temperature-sensitive switch that automatically controls home heating and air-conditioning systems. There are two types of thermostats used to control heating and air-conditioning systems. **Low-voltage thermostats** control whole-house heating and air conditioning from one central location. **Line-voltage thermostats** are used in zone heating systems, where each room has its own heating unit and thermostat.

A low-voltage thermostat is powered by a transformer that reduces 120-volt current to about 24 volts. A low-voltage thermostat is very durable, but failures can occur if wire connections become loose or dirty, if thermostat parts become corroded, or if a transformer wears out. Some thermostat systems have two transformers. One transformer controls the heating unit, and the other controls the air-conditioning unit.

Line-voltage thermostats are powered by the same circuit as the heating unit, usually a 240-volt circuit. Always make sure to turn off the power before servicing a line-voltage thermostat.

A thermostat can be replaced in about one hour. Many homeowners choose to replace standard low-voltage or line-voltage thermostats with programmable setback thermostats. These programmable thermostats can cut energy use by up to 35%.

When buying a new thermostat, make sure the new unit is compatible with your heating/air-conditioning system. For reference, take along the brand name and model number of the old thermostat and of your heating/air-conditioning units. When buying a new low-voltage transformer, choose a replacement with voltage and amperage ratings that match the old thermostat.

**Everything You Need:**

Tools: soft-bristled paint brush, multi-tester, screwdriver, combination tool, neon circuit tester, continuity tester.

Materials: masking tape, short piece of wire.

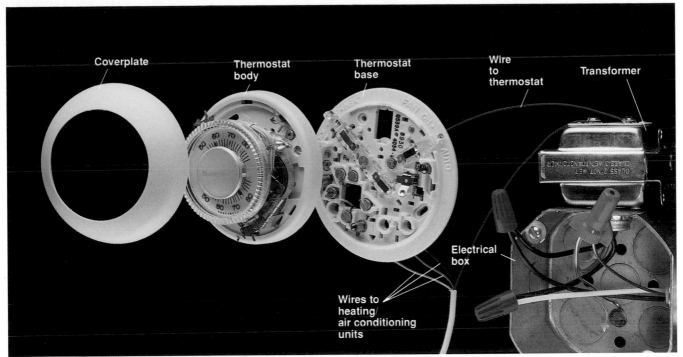

Coverplate    Thermostat body    Thermostat base    Wire to thermostat    Transformer

Electrical box

Wires to heating/ air conditioning units

**Low-voltage thermostat system** has a transformer that is either connected to an electrical junction box or mounted inside a furnace access panel. Very thin wires (18 to 22 gauge) send current to the **thermostat**. The thermostat constantly monitors room temperatures, and sends electrical signals to the heating/cooling unit through additional wires. The number of wires connected to the thermostat varies from two to six, depending on the type of heating/air-conditioning system. In the common four-wire system shown above, power is supplied to the thermostat through a single wire attached to screw terminal R. Wires attached to other screw terminals relay signals to the furnace heating unit, the air-conditioning unit, and the blower unit. Before removing a thermostat, make sure to label each wire to identify its screw terminal location.

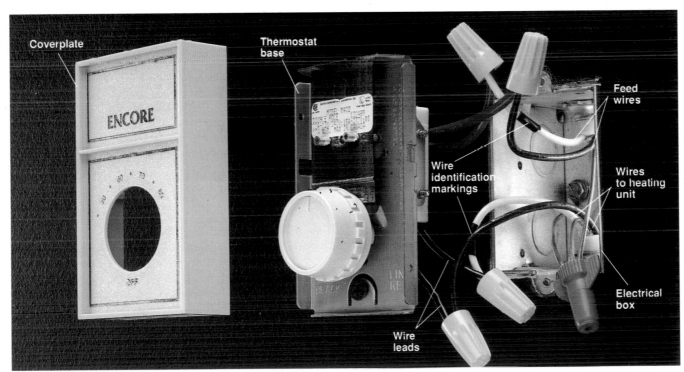

Coverplate    Thermostat base

Feed wires

Wire identification markings

Wires to heating unit

Electrical box

Wire leads

ENCORE

**Line-voltage thermostat** for 240-volt baseboard heating unit usually has four wire leads, although some models have only two leads. On a four-wire thermostat, the two red wire leads (sometimes marked LINE or L) are attached to the two hot feed wires bringing power into the box from the service panel. The black wire leads (sometimes marked LOAD) are connected to the circuit wires that carry power to the heating unit.

## How to Inspect & Test a Low-voltage Thermostat System

**Coverplate**

**1** Turn off power to the heating/air-conditioning system at the main service panel. Remove the thermostat coverplate.

**2** Clean dust from the thermostat parts using a small, soft-bristled paint brush.

**Mounting screws**

**3** Remove the thermostat body by loosening the mounting screws with a screwdriver.

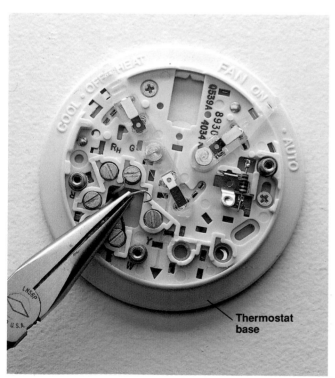

**Thermostat base**

**4** Inspect the wire connections on the thermostat base. Reattach any loose wires. If wires are broken or corroded, they should be clipped, stripped, and re-attached to the screw terminals (page 100).

**5** Locate the low-voltage transformer that powers the thermostat. This transformer usually is located near the heating/air-conditioning system, or inside a furnace access panel. Tighten any loose wire connections.

**6** Set the control dial of multi-tester meter to the 50-volt (AC) range. Turn on power to the heating/air-conditioning system at the main service panel.

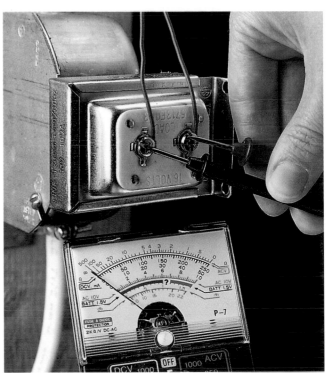

**7** Touch one probe of multi-tester to each of the low-voltage screw terminals. If tester does not detect current, then the transformer is defective and must be replaced (page 155).

**8** Turn on power to heating system. Set thermostat control levers to AUTO and HEAT.

**9** Strip ½" from each end of a short piece of insulated wire. Touch one end of the wire to terminal marked W and other end to terminal marked R. If heating system begins to run, then the thermostat is faulty and must be replaced (page 154).

# How to Install a Programmable Low-voltage Thermostat

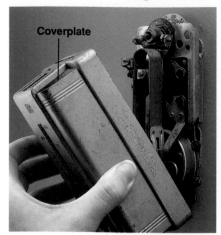

**1** Turn off the power to the heating/air-conditioning system at the main service panel. Remove the thermostat coverplate.

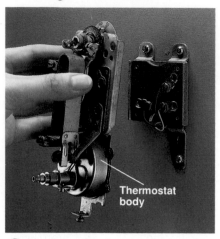

**2** Unscrew the thermostat mounting screws and remove the thermostat body.

**3** Label the low-voltage wires to identify their screw terminal locations, using masking tape. Disconnect all low-voltage wires.

**4** Remove the thermostat base by loosening the mounting screws. Tape the wires against the wall to make sure they do not fall into the wall cavity.

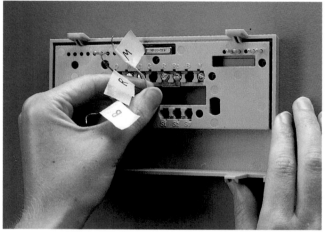

**5** Thread the low-voltage wires through base of new thermostat. Mount the thermostat base on the wall, using the screws included with the thermostat.

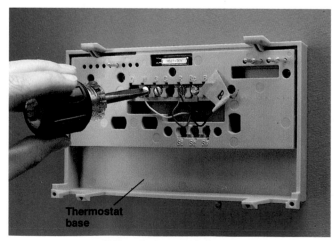

**6** Connect the low-voltage wires to the screw terminals on the thermostat base. Use the manufacturer's connection chart as a guide.

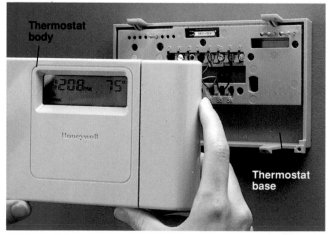

**7** Install batteries in thermostat body, then attach the body to thermostat base. Turn on power and program the thermostat as desired.

# How to Replace a Low-voltage Transformer

**1** Turn off the power to the heating/air-conditioning system at the main service panel. Remove the coverplate on the transformer electrical box.

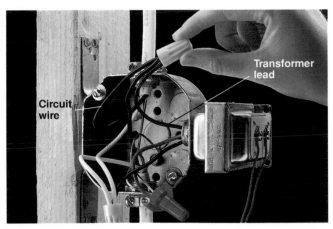

**2** Carefully remove the wire nut connecting the black circuit wire to the transformer lead. Be careful not to touch bare wires.

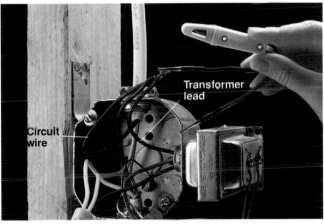

**3** Test for power by touching one probe of neon circuit tester to grounded metal box and other probe to exposed wires. Remove wire nut from white wires and repeat test. Tester should not glow for either test. If it does, power is still entering box. Return to service panel and turn off correct circuit.

**4** Disconnect the grounding wires inside the box, then disconnect low-voltage wires attached to the screw terminals on the transformer. Unscrew the transformer mounting bracket inside the box, and remove transformer. Purchase a new transformer with the same voltage rating as the old transformer.

**5** Attach new transformer to electrical box. Reconnect circuit wires to transformer leads. Connect circuit grounding wires to transformer grounding lead.

**6** Connect the low-voltage wires to the transformer, and reattach the electrical box coverplate. Turn on the power at the main service panel.

**1** Turn off the power to the heating unit at the main service panel. Remove the thermostat coverplate.

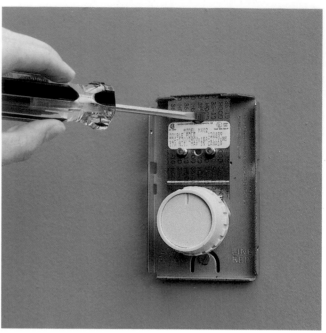

**2** Loosen the thermostat mounting screws, and carefully pull the thermostat from the electrical box.

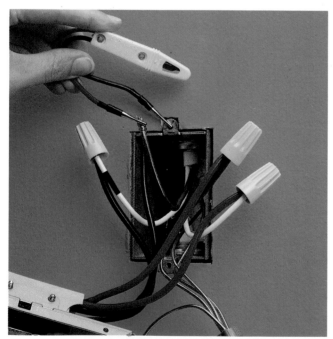

**3** Unscrew one wire nut. Test for power by touching one probe of neon circuit tester to grounded metal box and touching other probe to exposed wires. Tester should not glow. Repeat test with other wire connections. Tester should not glow. If it does, then power is still entering box. Return to service panel and turn off correct circuit.

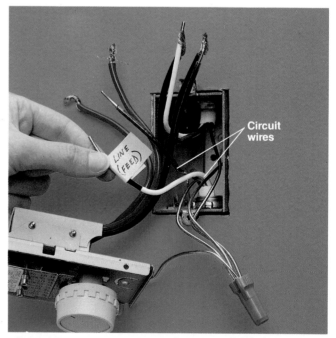

Circuit wires

**4** Identify the two circuit wires that are attached to the thermostat leads marked LINE. These leads are often red. The circuit wires attached to the LINE leads bring power into the box, and are known as feed wires. Label the feed wires with masking tape, then disconnect all wires.

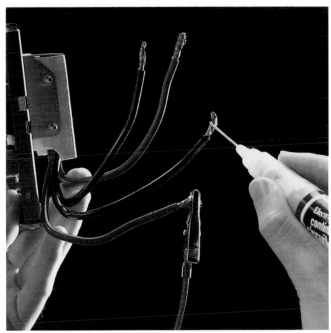

**5** Test thermostat by attaching the clip of a continuity tester to one of the red wire leads, then touching probe to black wire lead on same side of thermostat. Turn temperature dial from HIGH to LOW. Tester should glow in both positions. Repeat test with other pair of wire leads. If tester does not glow for both positions, thermostat is faulty and must be replaced.

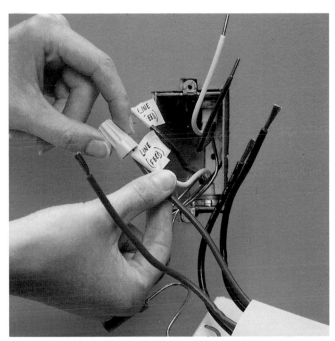

**6** Replace a faulty thermostat with a new thermostat that has the same voltage and amperage ratings as the old one. Connect the new thermostat by attaching the circuit feed wires to the wire leads marked LINE, using wire nuts.

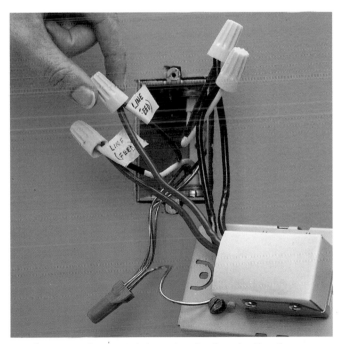

**7** Connect the remaining circuit wires to the thermostat leads marked LOAD, using wire nuts. Connect the grounding wires together with a wire nut.

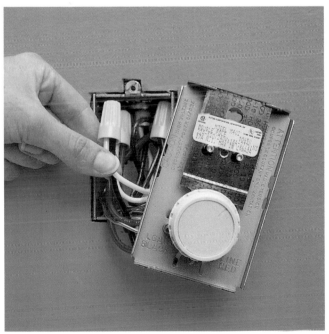

**8** Carefully fold the wires inside the electrical box, then attach the thermostat mounting screws and the coverplate. Turn on the power at the main service panel. If new thermostat is programmable (page 150), set the program as desired.

# Index